Women's Rights in the Quran

Ayatullah Misbah Yazdi

Translator
Zaid Alsalami

Originally published in the Farsi language.
This English edition is published in 2025.

ISBN: 978-1-7384949-7-2

© AIM Foundation 2025

All rights reserved. No part of this publication may be reproduced, stored in a retrieval system, or transmitted in any form or by any means, digital, electronic, mechanical, photocopying, recording, or otherwise, or conveyed via the internet or a website without prior written permission of the publisher, except in the case of brief quotations embodied in critical articles and reviews.

بسم الله الرحمن الرحيم

*In the name of God, the Merciful,
the Compassionate*

Contents

Translator's Preface 9
Introduction 15
The Creation of Women 19
    The Equality of Men and Women in Creation 19
    Differences Between a Male and a Female 30
    A Woman's Intellect 36
    The Preference of Men Over Women 39
    Verses Giving Impression of Men Being Better than Women 45
    Masculine Addressing in the Qurʾān and the Preference of Men 46
    Creational Distinctions and Legislative Differences 49
    Necessary Connection Between Creational and Legal Difference 54
The Philosophy of Women's Laws 59
    Women's Inheritance 63
    The Testimony of a Woman 65
Women's Civil Rights 69
    The Permissibility of Temporary Marriage and Polygamy 72
    Conditions for Polygamy in Islam 75
    The Permissibility of Divorce 77
    Legal and Moral Principles in a Family 78
    The Aims for the Establishment of a Family 84

   Family Stability 89
   Encouragement and Increase of Marriage 95
   Disciplining Women 99
Miscellaneous Issues **105**
   Women's Independence in Faith and Disbelief 105
   Controlling of Sexual Desire 107
   Morals of Women.. 111
   Special Rules for the Wives of the Prophet 116
   Feminism in the Modern World..118
   Outcomes of Movements Defending Women's Rights 119

Translator's Preface

Modernity has brought about many deviations and challenges with respect to how we see things. This is especially exacerbated with globalisation, social media, and the growth of Muslim 'communities' in predominantly non-Muslim societies. Numerous trends and ideologies try to alter our perspective and challenge what was once commonly seen to be natural and unquestionable. Such trends have resulted in the modification of laws and have also strongly influenced religion and religious people. It is expected that religious establishments accommodate these imposed views or else be branded as backward, archaic, discriminative, and oppressive.

One example is the issue of gender. It was commonly seen as being binary in nature—either male or female—but now has turned into a contentious and sensitive topic including individuals who do not identify as 'male' or 'female.' Such a simple topic has become so complex and controversial that gender identity is no longer defined as how one is born. Sexual orientation is also constantly evolving, the LGBTQIA2S+ movement being a prime example.[1] Furthermore, feminism with all its trends, has embedded itself in society, assuming it will bring about equal rights for women.

As followers of a divine religion, it is necessary to understand our position towards these trends in a setting that is untainted by outside influence or imposed views. As Muslims, it is our duty to honour our religion and preserve our Islamic worldview by obeying our Creator and following our scripture. As Shīʿī Muslims, we are privileged to have the Ahlul Bayt (a.s.) as our role models, who are the custodians of the Qurʾān and have given us the all-inclusive method of how we should live our lives.

We are bombarded with baseless accusations and negative portrayals of our religion, especially in the area of women rights. It is for this reason that this book is an important contribution to gender related topics and answering misconceptions frequently raised against Islam.

---

1. This is an acronym for 'Lesbian, Gay, Bisexual, Transgender, Queer/Questioning, Intersex, Asexual, Two-Spirit,' and the countless other affirmative ways in which people choose to self-identify themselves.

Translator's Preface

The present work, *Ḥuqūq-e Zan dar Qur'ān* (*Women's Rights in the Qur'ān*) is the fifth volume of the *Pursesh va Pāsukh-hā (Questions and Answers)* series and, is a compilation of excerpts from the various prolific works of the late Ayatullah Muhammad Taqi Misbah Yazdi (1935–2021). Ayatullah Misbah Yazdi was a revered scholar, professor of philosophy, and one of the most highly respected clerics in the Shīʿī world, seen as an esteemed authority in Islamic thought. He is famously known for his lucid approach in explaining Islam and addressing misconceptions and theological challenges in today's modern world. It was his institute, the Imām Khomeinī Educational and Research Institute, that delegated us the task of translating his book into English, which we completed back in 2007. Professor Muhammad Legenhausen was also involved in overseeing the project, and we are grateful for his guidance. Unfortunately, it was not published and so, we took it upon ourselves to prepare the text for publication.

It has gone through numerous hands for editing, proofreading, and reviewing. We were mainly interested for our fellow Muslim sisters, especially converts, to go through the text and give feedback and suggestions to render the work as beneficial as possible. Our joint aim was to keep the language simple for anyone to understand but also to stay loyal to the original Persian as much as possible. There are many sisters who generously contributed their time and effort, and to each we are humbly grateful. We cannot name them all, but we would like to specifically mention Sr. Yvette Baldacchino and Professor Therese Taylor

Zaid Alsalami

زيد الـسَّلامي

Translator's Preface

Introduction

One of the main issues attracting lively debate in today's society is the rights and status of women in Islamic thought. This topic has gained increasing coverage and burgeoning research, occupying a prominent place in publications, research, novels and more recently, social media.

The social movement advocating for the rights of women, commonly known as 'feminism,' was primarily formed in the West, and gradually found its way to other countries around the world, including Iran. This movement has significantly grown in the last couple of years. In order to promulgate and spread this movement, its proponents have used visual media, such as film and television, as well as books and publications.

That being said, it is important not to overlook the sinister intentions that linger behind the facade of this movement. Many who speak about the rights of women are in fact only seeking their own political agendas, and the outcome of their slogans will bring nothing but depravity and increased oppression towards women.

It is therefore necessary to present the Islamic view regarding this issue. Such a discussion will not only refute common misconceptions about Islam and gender, but also expose the corruption, false political plots, and deceptions existing in some feminist ideologies.

This book is a summary of various issues covered by an outstanding scholar and expert in the field of Islamic thought, the late Ayatullah Muhammad Taqi Misbah Yazdi, who has discussed topics related to gender and the rights of women in many of his writings and lectures.

It is presented in a question-and-answer format, divided into four chapters: (1) The Creation of Women; (2) The Philosophy of Women's laws; (3) Women's Civil Rights; and (4) Miscellaneous Issues.

We hope this significant work will assist its readers to better understand the issues related to the rights of women from an Islamic worldview, and by clarifying the details of this topic, some misconceptions and questions will be answered.

We would like to acknowledge and sincerely thank Hamīd Karimi for his efforts in compiling these discussions and Zaid Alsalami for translating it into English.

Imām Khomeinī Education and Research Institute

Publications Department

Qom, Iran

The Creation of Women

The Equality of Men and Women in Creation

QUESTION: It is said that according to Islam a woman is the 'branch,' a man is the 'origin,' and that the woman is inferior to man in humanity. Is this true?

ANSWER: The equal status of the male and female gender derives from the fact that they are both human beings and share the same human features. That being said, in logical terms, the male and female are also categorically different. Explaining their similarities and differences will help in understanding their rights and duties.

From a Qur'ānic perspective, it is possible to categorise the similar features of men and women as follows:[2]

1. The male and the female are similar in human essence and whatever else is related to it. This means that both are considered to be "human beings," but even though they have one specific unity as far as their species (*naw'*)[3] is concerned, they logically relate to two different genders. As obvious as this may be, a contesting theory has existed which states that women were not considered to be humans, and that they had a different essence.[4] Islam absolutely rejects this, as can be seen in the following Qur'ānic verse:

(يَا أَيُّهَا النَّاسُ اتَّقُوا رَبَّكُمُ الَّذِي خَلَقَكُمْ مِنْ نَفْسٍ وَاحِدَةٍ وَخَلَقَ مِنْهَا زَوْجَهَا)

---

2. Muḥammad-Taqī Miṣbāḥ Yazdī, *Ḥuqūq va Siyāsat dar Qur'ān*, lesson 26.

3. In logic, species (*naw'*) is one of the five universals. It refers to the common reality shared between a group of individuals, for example, humans.

4. "There were extensive debates on whether or not women could be considered human beings. For more details on this see: Jens Christian Bay, "Women not considered Human Beings: A Bibliological Curiosity," in *The Library Quarterly: Information, Community, Policy,* vol. 4, no. 2 (April 1934), pp. 164–156. Another interesting look into the struggle women had in defining who they are can be seen in: Catharine A. MacKinnon, *Are Women Human?: And Other International Dialogues* (Cambridge: Harvard University Press, 2006). We also know about the earlier British and North American constitutions where women were not classified as 'persons,' *per se.*

> *O Mankind! Be wary of your Lord who created you from a single soul, and created its mate from it.*[5]

The expression 'and created its mate from it,' clearly shows that Adam's pair, Eve, was from himself. Furthermore, both Adam and Eve were equally deceived by the whisperings of Satan, which in itself demonstrates that they were partners in their fate. A lot can be learned when we compare the Qur'ān and the Old Testament on the topic of Adam and Eve being deceived in the Garden of Eden. In parts 13–1 of chapter 3 of Genesis, it speaks about the serpent tempting and tricking Eve, and at the end it says:

> *...when the woman saw that the tree was good for food, and that it was pleasant to the eyes, and a tree to be desired to make one wise, she took of the fruit thereof, and did eat, and gave also unto her husband with her; and he did eat.*[6]

When Almighty God reproached Adam, Adam said,

> *The woman whom thou gavest to me, she gave me of the tree, and I did eat.*[7]

God then said to Eve,

---

5. Qur'ān, 1 :4.
6. Genesis, 6 :3.
7. Genesis, 12 :3.

> *"What is this that thou hast done?"*
>
> *The woman said, "The serpent beguiled me, and I did eat."*[8]

Based on this, Jews and Christians believe that Satan deceived Eve, and in turn she deceived Adam. As for Islam, in the three different places where the Qurʾān discusses the story of Adam and Eve,[9] Almighty God addresses both Adam and Eve equally and rebukes them both for being deceived and succumbing to Satan's temptation. Therefore, it is incorrect to claim that Eve was deceived by Satan, and Adam was deceived by Eve. Rather, it was Satan who tricked and deceived them equally and together.

2. In Islam, there is no distinction between men and women in their quest to achieve high levels of perfection. Both men and women are rewarded equally based on their acts of worship and devout submission to Almighty God. It is not the case whereby some aspects and degrees of human perfection are exclusively for men, and therefore unattainable for women, or vice versa.[10]

3. In the area of truth and falsity, men and women exist on each of the spectrums. It is an error to claim that

---

8. Genesis, 12 :3.
9. See: Qurʾān, 23–19 :7 ;36–35 :2; and 122–117 :20.
10. See: Qurʾān, ;12 :57 ;6–5 :48 ;35 :33 ;72 :9 ;97 :27 ;124 :4 ;221 :2 56 :36; and 8 :40.

truth or falsehood is more inclined to one gender and less to the other. It is either true faith or hypocrisy that places humans on the side of truth or falsehood, rather than simply being a woman or a man. Men and women who truly have faith and do good deeds are partners to each other,[11] and men and women who are disbelievers or hypocrites are also partners to each other.[12]

4. There are many duties and obligations men and women commonly share. In Qurʾānic verses, these duties are referred to in the form of the masculine pronoun[13] or in both the masculine and feminine pronouns.

(يَا أَيُّهَا الَّذِينَ آمَنُواْ كُتِبَ عَلَيْكُمُ الصِّيَامُ)

O you who have faith! Prescribed for you is fasting...[14]

In this verse, although masculine pronouns are used, it is not addressing only men but both genders. As a result, the verse means: O men and women with faith, fasting has become obligatory for you.

---

11. This is in reference to, "But the faithful men and women are allies (*awliyāʾ*) of one another." Qurʾān, 71:9.
12. Qurʾān, 71:9, 67–68 and 24:26.
13. Most verses of the Qurʾān, in their commands and prohibitions, address both the male and the female, even though it uses the masculine pronoun. The reason for usage of the masculine form goes back to the significance of the Arabic language and grammatical purpose.
14. Qurʾān, 2:183.

Among the verses that refer to both forms are:

(قُلْ لِلْمُؤْمِنِينَ يَغُضُّوا مِنْ أَبْصَارِهِمْ وَيَحْفَظُوا فُرُوجَهُمْ ذَلِكَ أَزْكَى لَهُمْ إِنَّ اللَّهَ خَبِيرٌ بِمَا يَصْنَعُونَ)

Tell the faithful men to cast down their gaze and to guard their private parts. That is more decent for them. Allah is indeed well aware of what they do.[15]

And:

(وَقُلْ لِلْمُؤْمِنَاتِ يَغْضُضْنَ مِنْ أَبْصَارِهِنَّ وَيَحْفَظْنَ فُرُوجَهُنَّ)

And tell the faithful women to cast down their gaze and to guard their private parts.[16]

In the same Surah, it says:

(الزَّانِيَةُ وَالزَّانِي فَاجْلِدُوا كُلَّ وَاحِدٍ مِنْهُمَا مِائَةَ جَلْدَةٍ)

As for the unmarried fornicatress and the fornicator, strike each of them a hundred lashes.[17]

In another verse, it says:

---

15. Qur'ān, 30 :24.
16. Qur'ān, 31 :24.
17. Qur'ān, 2 :24.

(وَالسَّارِقُ وَالسَّارِقَةُ فَاقْطَعُوا أَيْدِيَهُمَا جَزَاءً بِمَا كَسَبَا نَكَالاً مِنَ اللَّهِ)

As for the man-thief and woman-thief, cut off their hands as a requital for what they have earned [that is] an exemplary punishment from Allah.[18]

5. Islam rejects any form of discrimination or oppression based on gender. In the pre-Islamic era, the polytheist bedouins had certain customs and habits that were extremely oppressive towards females. An example of this, that has been strongly condemned in the Qurʾān, is their ritual of burying alive newborn females.[19] Another example is the practice of pre-Islamic Arabs declaring that the ownership of any newborn cattle that stays alive is exclusively for men and forbidden for women.

6. Just as men are independent in social and political activities, women also have their distinct social and political independence. They are both equal in terms of the rights of participation in all aspects of society, unless their distinct physical and psychological differences in accordance with divine judgment require otherwise. The Qurʾānic verses that give evidence to independence of women in social-political issues are:

---

18. Qurʾān, 38: 5.
19. Qurʾān, 59–58: 16 and 9–8: 81.

(يَا أَيُّهَا الَّذِينَ آمَنُوا إِذَا جَاءَكُمُ الْمُؤْمِنَاتُ مُهَاجِرَاتٍ فَامْتَحِنُوهُنَّ اللَّهُ أَعْلَمُ بِإِيمَانِهِنَّ فَإِنْ عَلِمْتُمُوهُنَّ مُؤْمِنَاتٍ فَلَا تَرْجِعُوهُنَّ إِلَى الْكُفَّارِ لَا هُنَّ حِلٌّ لَهُمْ وَلَا هُمْ يَحِلُّونَ لَهُنَّ وَآتُوهُمْ مَا أَنْفَقُوا وَلَا جُنَاحَ عَلَيْكُمْ أَنْ تَنْكِحُوهُنَّ إِذَا آتَيْتُمُوهُنَّ أُجُورَهُنَّ وَلَا تُمْسِكُوا بِعِصَمِ الْكَوَافِرِ وَسْأَلُوا مَا أَنْفَقْتُمْ وَلْيَسْأَلُوا مَا أَنْفَقُوا ذَلِكُمْ حُكْمُ اللَّهِ يَحْكُمُ بَيْنَكُمْ وَاللَّهُ عَلِيمٌ حَكِيمٌ)

O you who have faith! When faithful women come to you as immigrants, test them. Allah knows best [the state of] their faith. Then, if you ascertain them to be faithful women, do not send them back to the disbelievers. They [faithful women] are not lawful for them [infidel men], nor are they [infidel men] lawful for them [faithful women]. And give them what they have spent [for them]. There is no sin upon you in marrying them when you have given them their dowries. Do not hold onto [conjugal] ties with faithless women. Ask [the infidels] for what you have spent, and let the faithless ask for what they have spent. That is the judgment of Allah; He judges between you. And Allah is all-knowing, all-wise.[20]

And:

---

20. Qur'ān, 10:60.

(يَا أَيُّهَا النَّبِيُّ إِذَا جَاءَكَ الْمُؤْمِنَاتُ يُبَايِعْنَكَ عَلَىٰ أَن لَّا يُشْرِكْنَ بِاللَّهِ شَيْئًا وَلَا يَسْرِقْنَ وَلَا يَزْنِينَ وَلَا يَقْتُلْنَ أَوْلَادَهُنَّ وَلَا يَأْتِينَ بِبُهْتَانٍ يَفْتَرِينَهُ بَيْنَ أَيْدِيهِنَّ وَأَرْجُلِهِنَّ وَلَا يَعْصِينَكَ فِي مَعْرُوفٍ ۙ فَبَايِعْهُنَّ وَاسْتَغْفِرْ لَهُنَّ اللَّهَ ۖ إِنَّ اللَّهَ غَفُورٌ رَحِيمٌ)

O Prophet! If faithful women come to you to take the oath of allegiance, [pledging] that they shall not ascribe any partners to Allah, that they shall not steal, nor commit adultery, not kill their children, not utter any slander that they may have intentionally fabricated, not disobey you in what is right, then accept their allegiance, and plead for them to Allah for forgiveness. Indeed, Allah is all-forgiving, all-merciful.[21]

7. Like men, women have the right of ownership and are capable of being financially independent. In the West, until rather recently, women did not have any financial independence, whereas in the Islamic world and according to the teachings of the Qurʾān, women kept what they earned and had a share in inheritance as well.[22]

8. In the same way that fathers have a set of family rights, mothers also have rights, similar and in addition to the rights of a father. In designating rights allocated

---

21. Qurʾān, 12:60.
22. Qurʾān, 33–32:4.

to the parent, the natural influence of the father and the mother in the structure of a family, the birth of a child, facilitation of needs, education and upbringing are all taken into consideration. Without a doubt, the mother, who carries the child in her womb for nine months, and is then responsible for the breastfeeding, nursing and caring for the baby for the next two years, has a greater influence than the father, and therefore, must have additional rights. The Qur'ān and narrations stress the shared rights of parents but place greater emphasis on the rights of a mother. There are many narrations that mention the rights of a mother being above those of a father, like the famous narration stating that heaven lies under the feet of mothers,[23] and other astonishing commendations that are too many to be mentioned here.

Some Qur'ānic verses[24] speak about the shared rights between the father and the mother, for example:

(وَقَضَىٰ رَبُّكَ أَلَّا تَعْبُدُوا إِلَّا إِيَّاهُ وَبِالْوَالِدَيْنِ إِحْسَانًا ۚ إِمَّا يَبْلُغَنَّ عِنْدَكَ الْكِبَرَ أَحَدُهُمَا أَوْ كِلَاهُمَا فَلَا تَقُلْ لَهُمَا أُفٍّ وَلَا تَنْهَرْهُمَا وَقُلْ لَهُمَا قَوْلًا كَرِيمًا ۞ وَاخْفِضْ لَهُمَا جَنَاحَ الذُّلِّ مِنَ الرَّحْمَةِ وَقُلْ رَبِّ ارْحَمْهُمَا كَمَا رَبَّيَانِي صَغِيرًا)

---

23. *Mustadrak al-Wasāʾil*, v. 15, p. 180.
24. See: Qurʾān, 151 :6 ;36 :4 ;83 :2 ;8 :29; and 14 :19.

Your Lord has decreed that you shall not worship anyone except Him, and [He has enjoined] kindness to parents. Should they reach old age at your side – one of them or both – do not say to them, 'Fie!' And do not chide them, but speak to them noble words. Lower the wing of humility to them, out of mercy, and say, 'My Lord! Have mercy on them, just as they reared me when I was [a] small [child]!'[25]

Other verses mention the rights of a mother being far greater than that of a father, along with their reasons, such as:[26]

(وَوَصَّيْنَا الإِنْسَانَ بِوالِدَيْهِ إِحْسَاناً حَمَلَتْهُ أُمُّهُ كُرْهاً وَوَضَعَتْهُ كُرْهاً وَحَمْلُهُ وَ فِصَالُهُ ثَلاثُونَ شَهْراً)

We have enjoined man to be kind to his parents. His mother has carried him in travail, and bore him in travail, and his gestation and weaning take thirty months.[27]

Along with having shared rights as parents, the mentioning of the hardships of motherhood is an indication that her status and rights are greater than a father.

---

25. Qur'ān, 24–23 :17.
26. See: Qur'ān, 15–14 :31.
27. Qur'ān, 15 :46.

The common elements between a male and a female are much greater than what we have mentioned here. What we can conclude is that the male and the female are one and similar in their human essence, with no difference whatsoever between them in this regard.

Differences Between a Male and a Female

QUESTION: What are the important and primary differences between a male and a female that would correlate with their different rights and duties? Can it be said that there is no essential difference between a male and a female, other than their biological differences, and these external differences should not be the reason for differences in rights?

ANSWER: It is commonly known that a human being's intellect is not completely capable of comprehending all the details and particulars of these things. Therefore, the intellect must refer to divine legislation (*al-sharʿ*). This is because fundamentally the human being is incapable of knowing all the beneficial interests (*masāliḥ*) and detrimental harms (*mafāsid*) in their true realities, or else it would have designated its own moral and legal commandments and rules which would secure the happiness and true perfection for all of creation. If this was the case, there would be no need for revelation, prophethood and religion. The secret of mankind's continuous need for revelation and prophethood is because of the deficiency of the human intellect. Furthermore, the human mind is also not able to intellectually justify all divine laws and rules. Indeed, it is only Almighty God who has absolute knowledge of all beneficial interests and detrimental harms in all their reasons, details and precise particulars.

What we demonstrate in this discussion is that there are differences between a male and a female that constitute different effects in social life, and as a result, there are different social rights and duties. To further understand the particulars of the differences in rights and duties we must turn to divine legislation, because the meticulous issues within this topic are hidden from us, similar to how we do not know matters of the *shar'* in many other areas.

It is possible to divide the differences between a male and a female that would lead to different rights and rulings into two main categories:

a) Physical differences that can be perceived through sensual experience and known through physiology and anatomy.

b) Spiritual and psychological differences that are studied in psychology and can be perceived through sensual experience and intellectual analysis

The main aspects of the physical difference between a male and a female are:

1. Sexual organs: There is a difference between the sexual organs of a male and a female and a clear difference in the sex cells of a male (sperm) and the sex cells of a female (ovum). These obvious differences are the reasons why the involvement of a male in the reproduction of a baby is different and incomparable to that of a female. Furthermore, the natural duty of a female in reproduction is something that is exclusively limited to a woman and is outside of the capability of a man.

2. Difference in the structure of the chest area: A female's breasts are made in such a way that makes it easy for a newborn to feed, and hence the responsibility of breastfeeding and nurturing the baby is naturally given to the mother. The holy Qurʾān has given emphasis on this, mentioning the mother's role in the first two years of the newborn's life.[28]

---

28. Qurʾān, 15: 46, 15–14: 31, 233: 2

3. Women's monthly menstrual cycle: The divine wisdom of Almighty God made the structure of a female in such a way that for a few days in every month she discharges some of her blood. During this period, a woman might feel unwell and become physically weak. Another regular symptom females experience during this period is a difference in their mood and emotions, and as a result, a woman would be in need of rest. Men do not experience such a thing.

4. Sexual needs and the ability of reproduction: When a woman becomes pregnant until the time she gives birth, and in most cases, even during the time the child is being breastfed, she is not able to become pregnant again. During this time, a woman's sexual desire decreases, whereas the sex drive of a man in most circumstances does not cease. The sexual organ of a woman usually only produces one mature egg once a month and it is ready to fertilise for a short time. This is why during the time of reproduction the sexual needs of a woman are different to that of a man.

5. Physical stamina: This difference is evident and is acknowledged by statistics and scientific research as well. Statistics show that the physical strength of a male is more than the physical strength of a female. The ability to tolerate hard work is a lot higher in men than in women. A man's body is rougher and more durable, and a woman's body is generally softer and gentler.

The most important spiritual and psychological differences between a male and a female are:

1. The female is subject to more emotions, reactions and feelings: These psychological features are generally the reason that women are more affectionate and express more loving behaviour. These characteristics make a female laugh, cry and have other reactions quicker than a male. The female's additional affection is also the cause for her extra care, love, soft heartedness, motherly emotions, and so on.

One of the outcomes of these differences is a relative lack of determination and at times, lack of broader thinking. Her feelings and emotions take away the power of assessment, broader thinking and correct judgment, and a female is normally under this influence during most periods of her life. Her emotional spirit weakens her power of management and supervision of the intellect, and this is why her judgments are at times trivial and unpractical. This difference has a major effect in the topic of women becoming rulers, judges and assuming managerial roles.

Such distinctive physiological features bring about many beneficial and useful results in their required areas. Taking up many crucial duties requires a lot of emotions and extra fragility, and when women perform such duties, they are more successful at them.

For example, parenting, feeding children, cleaning, washing, playing and taking care of the child, fulfilling its emotional needs and so on are all things that are compatible with a woman's innate disposition, whereas most men are not like this. Psychologists and especially female psychologists confirm this reality.

2. Women's inclination towards being loved and desire to receive attention: Another important difference is a woman's desire for being loved and cared for. In contrast, a man inclines towards giving love and care. One of the psychological needs of a woman is to seize the heart of a man and set his attention towards her, whereas a man tries to set his heart on her and love her. Men are normally the lovers and women the ones who are loved.

A very interesting point is that the Creator has placed the power of attracting hearts in women. It cannot be that a woman hunts for hearts but does not have the snare and bait. Furthermore, Allah (swt), who has given women the quality of being attractive, has also given men the capability of being attracted.

3. The strong urge of women to display and show themselves: One of the concerns of the female gender is that she shows herself off in front of others with any physical trait or material items in her possession. She beautifies herself and with cleverness tries to display her

beauty and decorations to others, especially to men, in order to catch their attention.

4. The need for women to be protected: Another spiritual difference between woman and man is a woman's need to be protected. On the other hand, it is in the nature of man to protect others. In other words, women like to resort to men for protection and men feel content when women seek refuge in them.

There are other physical and spiritual differences between the male and female, but they are less important, and so we will not be mentioning them.

The physical and psychological differences spoken about here are the reason for the fundamental differences in a man and woman's individual, family and social life. Therefore, it is of absolute necessity to pay attention to this when allocating rights and duties. Understanding these differences will help us to establish and uphold a divinely guided family system and preserve the human generation

A Woman's Intellect

QUESTION: It is said that a woman's brain is smaller than that of a man, and a man has more intellectual strength than a woman. In some traditions (*hadith*) such expressions have been mentioned which have resulted in some to conclude that the intellectual faculty of women is weak. Can it be said that a woman's intellect is less than a man's, and would this be regarded as a deficiency for women?

ANSWER: With respect to the issue of the natural differences between a man and woman,[29] there are differences that have been mentioned but do not seem to be that accurate. For example, it is said that a woman's brain is smaller than a man's brain. If this can be established, then it would explain the psychological differences in the areas of knowledge and awareness. It has also been said that the abilities of understanding, perception and reasoning are present less in a woman than a man. For us, these claims have not yet been proven. The traditions that have been narrated in this regard are not very clear and certain explanations have been mentioned for each one of them.

Statistical psychological research shows that the capability of women to comprehend some sciences and ideas, such as those in the mathematical and philosophical fields is weaker than that of men. They also claim that a woman's intelligence[30] is less than

---

29. Muhammad Taqi Misbah Yazdi, *Juzveye Huqūq va Siyāsat dar Qur'ān*, lesson 209.
30. The intellectual ability or the IQ is relating the intellectual age

that of a man. However, we believe this issue is still not clear and needs to be further researched and discussed. Is 'intelligence' a word for one faculty or a name for a group of a few faculties and potentials, like memory, quick transference, and depth in comprehending things? The issue of comprehending and understanding has multiple dimensions and psychologists call these different aspects one name: intelligence. It could be that it is not possible to compare the usage of the intellect of a man and a woman, because in some parts of learning and teaching, a woman could be stronger and in other parts, a man could be stronger. Nonetheless, the proving of these issues is not definite, and even if they were, they are not something that needs to be paid attention to.

What should be paid attention to is the fact that because a woman has strong emotions and feelings, her ability to reason and analyse are dampened, and because setting emotions and feelings aside is the first condition for correct thinking, a woman in this aspect is liable to more mistakes. As for man –in so far as he has weaker emotions and feelings- it is easier for him to think logically and make judgements. Therefore, it can be said that the intellectual power of a man is stronger, but this strength is not derived from man himself, but

---

of an individual with his actual age and multiplying it by a hundred.

rather it is because emotions and feelings are weak in him.

In conclusion, men in general have the capability of intellectualising and management, and this is the reason for the differences in rights and duties between men and women.. Of course, when we make a comparison between man and woman, no particular man or woman is meant, rather it is the general nature of women and men that we are referring to, and these universal principles can have exceptions.

The Preference of Men Over Women

QUESTION: Some Qur'ānic verses and traditions give evidence to the creational (*takwīnī*) and legislative (*tashrīʿī*) differences between man and woman which highlight a level of preference, for example the verses:

(وَلِلرِّجَالِ عَلَيْهِنَّ دَرَجَةٌ ۗ وَٱللَّهُ عَزِيزٌ حَكِيمٌ)

And men have a degree above them[31]

And:

(ٱلرِّجَالُ قَوَّٰمُونَ عَلَى ٱلنِّسَآءِ)

---

31. Qur'ān, 228: 2.

> *Men are the managers of the women....*[32]

Doesn't the existence of such differences bring oppression to women?

ANSWER: The majority who pose this problem as a paradox are those who suppose women are oppressed and are trying to defend women's rights. However, our answer negates the oppression of both women and men. In answering, we will separate the creational and the legislative differences and shortly speak about each of them:

A. The creational system: Justice and oppression are primarily spoken about within the context of rights. Something cannot have rights unless it exists, such as the right to request its creator to either create it or not create it or to create it with a particular set of features. In other words, no existent can object to the original form it was created in or how it was created, as there are no rights for something that has not been created yet. No creation can protest against Allah (swt), by saying: Why did You create me and bring me out from non-existence? Why did You create me as a human and not a plant, a male and not a female, or the opposite? Why did You give me two eyes and not one or three? Why didn't you

---

32. Qur'ān, 34:4.

give me a stronger memory or intelligence, and other questions similar to this.

The giving of existence and allocating its limits are all in the hands of Allah Almighty. He creates what He wills and how He wills according to His perfect wisdom.

The creational differences between the different genera, categories and types are necessary in the system of creation and are in the interest and benefit of all creation. Therefore, in the origin of the creation of existents and the special characteristics each one has been given, we cannot speak about rights, justice, and oppression.

B. The legislative system: In legislation, it is possible that justness and oppression can exist on three levels.

1. On the level of duty.

2. On the level of judgement.

3. On the level of giving reward or punishment.

Any of the Qur'ānic verses that either verify the justness of Allah Almighty or negate oppression from Him point to one of these three categories.

If Allah (swt) places a duty upon someone who does not have the capability of doing it or the duty is given to someone with nothing in return, then in both circumstances there will be oppression on the level of duty.

If Allah (swt), after allocating just duties to human beings according to his wisdom (*ḥikmah*), assigned a reward or a punishment which is not appropriate for the action that was done, then there would be oppression on the level of judgement and allocation of reward and punishment.

Lastly, if Allah (swt), after fairly assigning the reward or punishment, does not give reward to the righteous or punish the wrongdoers, or if he were to punish the good and reward the bad, we can say that oppression has been done on the level of rewarding and punishing.

Now, we ask: Which one of these three categories of oppression has Allah performed on women or men?

It is not hard to perceive that Allah does not practice any oppression in the second and third category. If there is confusion in understanding whether He commits oppression, then it would be in the first category (the level of duty).

In order to understand this matter, we will refer to the Qurʾān. In verse 228 of Surah al-Baqarah, we read:

The Creation of Women

(وَلَهُـنَّ مِثْـلُ الَّـذِي عَلَيْهِـنَّ بِالْمَعْـرُوفِ ۚ وَلِلرِّجَـالِ عَلَيْهِـنَّ دَرَجَـةٌ...)

The wives have rights similar to the obligations upon them, in accordance with honourable norms; and men have a degree above them....[33]

The meaning of the first sentence in the verse is that the rights and duties of women are equivalent to each other. This is an ongoing universal principle, that is, whenever a right is assigned to a person, an appropriate duty is also put with that right; the vice versa also holds true. The beginning of the verse explicitly points to this, saying when there are duties allocated for women, then rights appropriate to those duties are also allocated so that they would not be oppressed (oppression on the level of duty), and this very rule is also applied to men.

The issue of importance here is that the parity of rights and duties of women and men is one thing, and the equality and similarity of man and woman is something else. The holy Qur'ān accepts the first and rejects the second. If, according to the extra strength and capability that is naturally bestowed in a man, heavier duties and responsibilities are given to him, then he will not be oppressed on the level of duty. Now, if according to these duties and responsibilities more rights and distinctions are allocated to a person, then again without doubt

---

33. Qur'ān, 2: 228.

oppression will not be done because the balance between rights and duties has been observed.

From another perspective, no oppression has been done to women if, according to her weaker ability, she is requested to perform lighter duties and has less rights, which are appropriate with the duties she is assigned. So far, the issue at hand is clear, but if we were to compare the extra rights of men in comparison to what is ordained for women, it is possible to suppose that oppression has been done. Whereas, if men had less rights (keeping in mind the balance between rights and duties, and duties and abilities) then it would be oppression to the man. Therefore, the preference of man over woman on the level of religious law (*tashrī'*) is (like on the level of nature/creation) not oppression, but rather it is absolute justice.

The interesting point observed in this verse is that there is no explanation as to the reason why preference is given to the male. From the explanations that were mentioned in the other questions, it becomes clear that the capability of a man in the fields of rationalising, management, physical work and economics are greater. According to this natural difference, the duty of managing life, family and expenses and the right of administration and decision making in family (and social) affairs has been given to men. Therefore, with reference to the holy verse 'Men are the managers of the women'³⁴ the meaning of 'degree' in the holy verse 'And men have a degree above them'³⁵ becomes clear.

Verses Giving Impression of Men Being Better than Women

QUESTION: Some Qurʾānic verses,³⁶ like verses 22-21 of Surah al-Najm say:

(أَلَكُمُ ٱلذَّكَرُ وَلَهُ ٱلْأُنثَىٰ ۞ تِلْكَ إِذًا قِسْمَةٌ ضِيزَىٰٓ)

*Are you to have males and He females? That, then, will be an unfair division.*³⁷

In this verse the polytheists are rebuked, asking them why it is that even though they loved their sons, they regarded angels to be the daughters of Allah. If a girl was equal to a boy, then why does Allah refuse this division in the verse and regard it as oppression?

ANSWER: The Qurʾān believes in the art of discussion and dialogue. It uses this method, utilizing what the opponents and adversaries accept as an argument

---

34. Qurʾān, 34 :4.
35. Qurʾān, 228 :2.
36. Refer to the Qurʾān, 39 :52, 19-16 :43, 157-149 :37, 62, 59-57 :16.
37. Qurʾān, 22-21 :53.

in order to respond to them. What is meant in the mentioned verse is in reality, in the form of debating (*jadal*), and not an argument (*burhān*), meaning to convict the polytheists according to what they acknowledge and not according to what is correct from the Qur'ānic viewpoint.

The preference of a boy and a man over a girl and a woman is something the polytheists regarded as an acceptable value. The holy Qur'ān shows the polytheists that according to their undisputed principle, they are refuted, and what they say is oppression, for, as previously stated, the Qur'ān denounces any kind of belief that views the woman to be inferior to man..

Masculine Addressing in the Qur'ān and the Preference of Men

QUESTION: Why are verses in the Qur'ān mainly addressed to the male gender? Does the Qur'ān give preference to the man by doing so?

ANSWER:[38] An introduction must be given in order to clarify the answer to this question: In some languages, like Persian, there are no differences between men and

---

38. Misbah Yazdi, *Juzveye Huqūq va Siyāsat dar Qur'ān*, lesson 206.

women and the masculine and feminine in regards to grammar and syntax. However, in Arabic and other languages, there is a difference, which manifests itself in verbs, pronouns, demonstrative adjectives, conjunctional nouns and adjectives. Therefore, when it is only men that are being addressed masculine tenses (*sighah*) are used and if the conversation is directed to women, then feminine tenses are used. Now, if the speech is about both men and women, what should be done? The answer is that, in Arabic, the masculine formula is used. In other words, in Arabic the masculine tense is used in two places:

When only men are being spoken about.

When a group of both men and women are being spoken about.

According to this principle, if we were to say that all (men and women) must be righteous and pious, we have no alternative other than to say it in the following way: "So let them be wary of Allah."[39] As a fair reader would see, the sentence is structured in such a way that no evaluation preference is involved. Therefore, there is no basis to think that preference is given to men over women. The holy Qurʾān does not go against the Arabic rules, and hence expressions like 'O you who have faith

---

39. Qurʾān, 9:4.

'يــا ايهــا الذيــن آمنــوا' cannot mean 'O those men who have faith,' rather it should be taken as 'O you who have faith,' including both men and women. Furthermore, it has never been heard that a woman or a man complained about a Qurʾānic verse at its time of revelation with respect to why it was only speaking about men and had given little to no concern to women. Nor was it ever asked if a divine law, Qurʾānic order or prohibition was specifically for men or if it included women as well.

What has been mentioned here is in regards to some Qurʾānic verses. Other parts are directly addressed to men only, like verses that speak about white skinned women with black eyes which are from the blessings of the Hereafter that the pure and pious men will be fortunate to get, or the verse [40] that says:

(أُحِلَّ لَكُمْ لَيْلَةَ الصِّيَامِ الرَّفَثُ إِلَىٰ نِسَائِكُمْ ۚ هُنَّ لِبَاسٌ لَكُمْ وَأَنتُمْ لِبَاسٌ لَهُنَّ ۗ...)

You are permitted, on the night of the fast, to go to your wives: they are a garment for you, and you are a garment for them...[41]

How can these forms of addressing be justified? The answer is that in the early days of Islam and in an ideal community of this religion, men were and are present in

---

40. Qurʾān, 22: 56, 20: 52, 54: 44.
41. Qurʾān, 187: 2.

the social field more than women. This is because men were more effective than women in these matters. In conclusion, such speech and action is pointing towards them, and this is especially true when it is directed to a prophet, who is a man.

However, this does not mean that superiority is for the man, and women are weaker or less than their counterparts. The real reason for such speeches is that the Prophet is naturally speaking mainly to the men of the society.

Creational Distinctions and Legislative Differences

QUESTION: What is the reason that creational and natural differences become the basis for social and legal differences? Can we say that women and men have creational and natural differences and so their duties and legal laws should be different?

ANSWER:[42] Men and women have similarities in creation, which bring about the grounds for similar laws. At the same time, their creational differences bring about

---

42. Misbah Yazdi, *Huqūq va Siyāsat dar Qurʾān*, lesson 208.

a series of distinctions and differences in legislative laws (individual or social).

The origin of this question comes from the known theory: The 'conclusion of 'ought' from what actually 'is." It was primarily the Western thinkers that used this discussion, presented first by the Scottish philosopher David Hume (1771-1711). Hume and his followers believe that the moral and legal 'ought' and 'ought not' cannot be derived from creational 'is' and 'is not,' and moral and legal philosophers must try to avoid committing such fallacies.

Natural distinctions can therefore never allow rights and duties to be different. This misconception, which is originally philosophical, or rather logical, can be applied to different sciences and needs to be comprehensively discussed. But we will only summarise the discussion to prepare an appropriate understanding of the different duties and rights of men and women.

The misconception can be put forward in the following logical formula: In the conclusion of an analogy, it is impossible to use a word that was not used in the first two premises, and therefore, it is impossible for the conclusion to have 'ought' and 'ought not,' putting them to the premises that have existence and non-existence. Therefore, how can it be logically correct that 'ought' be derived from 'what is?'

The summary of the answer is: Every proposition that is like the 'musts/existences' always has a part by the name of 'matter' that is not mentioned. This part can be necessary, possible, or impossible. If a proposition explains the cause and the effect relationship – like a conditional proposition in which the occurrence of the condition is the absolute cause for the occurrence of that part of the condition - the matter of that proposition will be necessary by analogy. This means the existence of the effect within the cause is necessary by analogy. The matter of the proposition in the conclusion of the logical analogy can come in the form of the expression 'ought,' and in such circumstances the 'must' that comes in the conclusion of the analogy is not something that did not come in one of the two premises. So, for example: The mixture of oxygen and hydrogen (with a known percentage and with certain circumstances) becomes the cause for the existence of water. This can also be explained in a conditional form by saying: 'If oxygen is mixed with hydrogen then water will be made.' We then add this sentence: 'however the water has been made.' In this case an exceptional syllogism in which its conclusion is: 'Oxygen and hydrogen must have been mixed together.'

The necessity that came in the conclusion explains the necessary analogy that came from the connection of the absolute cause (the mixture of oxygen and hydrogen) with the effect (water), deduced from the conditional proposition.

This matter is not restricted to only one science; rather it exists in all sciences like mathematics, physics, theology, logic, morals and law. Therefore, it is incorrect if we say that whenever the philosophers of morals and law derive the 'oughts' from the 'is,' they have fallen into a fallacy. For example, in law the adding of the case 'if social laws and duties are completely observed, there will be social happiness' with 'however, social happiness is required,' there will be an analogy in which the conclusion is: 'It is necessary to completely observe social laws and duties.' We can see that in the conditional proposition and in the major premise of the analogy, 'ought' does not exist, rather there is only a connection between the condition and its answer. Nonetheless, in the conclusion of the analogy an 'ought' comes into existence without us making a logical mistake. The 'oughts' that exist in morals are also the same as the oughts that exist in laws. Of course, it must be noted that the necessity that is acquired from the necessary analogy in which we are speaking about is in regards to the absolute cause and its effect. Therefore, it is not so that every conditional proposition has to conclude with an ought. In the cases where the absolute cause is not used and the occurrence of the condition is not the absolute cause of the occurrence of its answer, the conclusion of the 'ought' from the 'is' is a fallacy.

Clear invalid examples that the opposers use in concluding that 'ought' comes from 'is' in order to show its weakness are all because causality is absent in these cases and if not absent, it is a deficient cause. An example for this is the fallacious argument that the difference in the colour of people's skin is proof to their different rights and a justification for discrimination of races. But this comes from the colour of skin not being the absolute cause for any rights or duties, and if the skin colour was truly an absolute cause then the former example would not be a fallacy.

It is therefore important to say, using the language of law, that: The rights and duties of people must be allocated according to interests and depravations, and hence this will certainly bring about difference in rights and duties, or else there would not be a reason for difference. Therefore, the difference that exists in 'oughts' in the area of rights and other areas leads to difference in 'what should be.'

Necessary Connection Between Creational and Legal Difference

QUESTION: Is it necessary to put down different laws and rules for every issue where there is difference in creation among humans? Primarily, what are the kinds of differences between men and women that lead to differences in rights? Is there a core distinction between men and women?

ANSWER: Without doubt, human beings are physically and psychologically different from each other, to the extent that even two brothers can never be the same in all physical and psychological traits.

Most of these physical and psychological differences are more or less the reason for diverse social effects. From this perspective, the legislator has only three ways to legislate laws: Either all differences are taken into consideration or no differences are taken into consideration, or some are and some are not. If all differences are taken into consideration and a special law is set down according to every difference, then there must be a group of personal laws for every individual. It's clear that this is neither practical nor beneficial. If all differences were disregarded and all people submitted to one law and all rights and duties were the same for everyone, then the interests of the society would never be achieved. Therefore, the third way must be chosen where some differences are taken into consideration and the rest are disregarded. A question arises here: What kinds of differences must become the cause for differences in laws and what kinds must not.

In order for the creational differences to become the reason for distinct rules and regulations, they must have the following three characteristics:

Permanent: Since rules and regulations cannot continuously change, only the permanent and fixed differences should be taken into consideration.

Predominant and general: A difference should not be specified to one, two or a certain amount of people. The legislator cannot put down an individual set of laws for every member of society. The job of a legislator is nothing other than to put down laws for the whole or a relatively large class of society. If a large percentage of society has a particular characteristic, there can then be a specific law allocated for them because of the particular characteristic they all share.

Influence on social affairs: The differences that do not have an effect on social activities or in the quantity and quality of a person's participation should not be taken into consideration. For example, if the difference in skin colour is effective in the outcome of social activities, then it would be correct to allocate a set of laws for each and every race. However, it is not the case that a particular colour or race has the power to affect society more than others.

Men and women have certain creational differences which instigate different rights and duties. In any society throughout history, the differences between men and women are of three characteristics:

First: Fixed and permanent, because it's seldom that throughout human history a difference in the male or female gender has occurred where a man becomes a woman or a woman becomes a man. This difference will stay for the entirety of a person's life.

Second: General, because each of the two genders amount to approximately half of human society.

Third: They are the origin of the different effects in social life, as will be explained later.

Therefore, it is rational, correct and just that – regardless of mutual rights and duties, which are according to natural and creational similarities- men and women are different in the rest of the rights and duties they are given. If the difference of men and women in rights and duties are completely observed, women, men, and society's interests will be observed. On the other hand, if the difference of men and women in rights and duties are not observed, women, men, and society's interests will be neglected.

The Philosophy of Women's Laws

Question: What are the legal and legislative differences between men and women and which of these differences have been mentioned in the Qurʾān?

Answer:[43] As previously mentioned, men and women have biological and psychological differences which necessitate differences in rights and laws. These can be divided into three categories:

1. Difference in individual rights

2. Difference in family rights

3. Difference in social rights

---

43. Misbah Yazdi, *Huqūq va Siyāsat dar Qurʾān*, lesson 209.

Individual differences:[44] For example, every month a woman (during her menses) does not pray for a few days or fast; there is no such exemption for men. There are no Qur'ānic verses that mention individual differences, however, the traditions of the Infallibles (*Ma'ṣūmīn*), explain such differences between men and women.

With respect to family differences, there are more than eighty verses in the holy Qur'ān.[45] Considering that there are only two Qur'ānic verses regarding social differences, we can clearly see that the majority of legislative and legal differences between women and men mentioned in the Qur'ān point to family issues, which in of itself shows the importance of this social pillar.

There are two verses in the Qur'ān that mention the social differences between women and men:

1. The verse that says that prophethood is specifically for men:

(وَمَا أَرْسَلْنَا مِن قَبْلِكَ إِلَّا رِجَالًا نُوحِي إِلَيْهِم مِّنْ

---

44. Individual differences are categorised under legislative and legal differences and not under difference in rights in their specific meaning (family and social rights).
45. About twenty verses in Surah al-Baqarah, twenty verses in Surah al-Nisā' and approximately forty verses in other chapters.

(...أَهْلِ ٱلْقُرَىٰ)

We did not send [any apostles] before you except as men to whom We revealed from among the people of the towns....[46]

2. The verse that mentions that the witnessing and testimony of two women is equal to the witnessing and testimony of one man:

(وَاسْتَشْهِدُوا شَهِيدَيْنِ مِن رِّجَالِكُمْ ۖ فَإِن لَّمْ يَكُونَا رَجُلَيْنِ فَرَجُلٌ وَامْرَأَتَانِ مِمَّن تَرْضَوْنَ مِنَ الشُّهَدَاءِ أَن تَضِلَّ إِحْدَاهُمَا فَتُذَكِّرَ إِحْدَاهُمَا الْأُخْرَىٰ ۚ...)

And take as witness two witnesses from your men and if there are not two men, then a man and two women —from those whom you approve as witnesses— so that if one of the two defaults, the other will remind her.[47]

There are other differences in rights between men and women in society, which are mentioned in our traditions, including:

1. Initial/offensive (*ibtidā'ī*) Jihad specified for men: A woman has not been ordered to participate in offensive Jihad, meaning it is not obligatory on her.

---

46. Qur'ān, 109: 12, and also 7: 21, 43: 16.
47. Qur'ān, 282: 2.

2. The precedence of men over women in defensive Jihad: As long as there are enough men, it is not obligatory for women to participate in defensive Jihad. The only time Jihad becomes obligatory on women is when there is a need for them to participate. Therefore, the responsibility of defence is primarily on men.

3. Government: It is nearly a consensus among Shīʿite jurists that a woman cannot govern and lead the people. It is possible that this could also be the reason behind the Qurʾān specifying prophethood for men, because prophethood is a kind of leadership and management of the society.

4. Taking the responsibility of the judiciary: The majority of Shīʿah jurists say that being a judge is specific for men.

5. Being a Marjaʿ taqlīd: This is also an issue that the majority of Shīʿah jurists agree upon, but there are some who give the possibility of women being able to be a Marjaʿ taqlīd, but only as an explainer of divine laws and not in the position people return to for their religious issues nor for religious leadership of the society.

Women's Inheritance

Question: Why is a man's inheritance two times more than a woman's? Is this not discrimination and oppression to women?

Answer:[48] This point is repeatedly mentioned in the legal system of Islam.[49] There are parts of the branches and derivative sections of inheritance where the portion of man and woman is different, so much so that they are sometimes equal to each other. Moreover, there are some rare circumstances where the portion of a woman is more than that of a man, and hence it is not so that a man's portion is always more than a woman's inheritance.

In reality, inheritance is a capital that can be utilized in different economic areas to make the economical wheels of the society move quicker, bringing for its owner gains and profits. Therefore, if a man and woman's share is equal, then only half of the economical and financial capital of the society will be in constant circulation, because women usually cannot be active in economic matters the same way men can.

Moreover, a man has a lot of expenditures: The wife's nuptial gift (*ṣidāq/mahr*), living expenditures of

---

48. Misbah Yazdi, *Huqūq va Siyāsat dar Qurʾān*, lesson 211.
49. Qurʾān, 4:4.

all family members, paying a woman's wages for her breastfeeding, nursing children and taking care of the house (if she was to ask for wages), and other such things, whereas a woman is not responsible to spend anything. In order to have an adequate earning to fulfil all these expenditures, a man must have a larger capital to work with in order to be able to spend that money. Therefore, a larger portion of inheritance will help a man achieve this objective.

In conclusion, a man's share of inheritance must be larger than that of a woman's in order to preserve the wealth of the society, and so a man is capable of upholding the responsibilities of the family's expenditures. We should bear in mind that there might be other reasons for this law that we do not have knowledge of. Therefore, no oppression is done to women in regards to inheritance. Rather it's the opposite. Most of the profit that a man gains from the capital will go back to the woman, and a woman can use her capital and gain profits from it for herself.

It is worth mentioning that in many societies (past or present) women did not receive any share in inheritance. In some societies women were included along with money as inheritance. However, Islam and the Qur'ān clearly say that, not only is a woman not inherited, she gets inheritance like a man, but for certain reasons her share is different.

The Qur'ān says:

> (لِّلرِّجَالِ نَصِيبٌ مِّمَّا تَرَكَ الْوَالِدَانِ وَالْأَقْرَبُونَ وَلِلنِّسَاءِ نَصِيبٌ مِّمَّا تَرَكَ الْوَالِدَانِ وَالْأَقْرَبُونَ مِمَّا قَلَّ مِنْهُ أَوْ كَثُرَ ۚ نَصِيبًا مَّفْرُوضًا)
>
> *Men have a share in the inheritance left by parents and near relatives, and women have a share in the inheritance left by parents and near relatives, whether it be little or much, a share ordained [by Allah].*[50]

The rest of this Qur'ānic chapter mentions the different cases and divisions of inheritance. The shares of the children, son and daughter, brother and sister, the mother and father, husband and wife, have all been specified.

The Testimony of a Woman

Question: Why is the testimony of two women equal to that of one man, and why is it that principally a man should be a witness?

Answer:[51] According to some verses in the Qur'ān, the testimony of two women is equal to the testimony of one man. In verse 282 of Surah al-Baqarah, it says:

---

50. Qur'ān, 7:4.
51. Misbah Yazdi, *Huqūq va Siyāsat dar Qur'ān*, lesson 210.

> (وَاسْتَشْهِدُوا شَهِيدَيْنِ مِن رِّجَالِكُمْ ۖ فَإِن لَّمْ يَكُونَا رَجُلَيْنِ فَرَجُلٌ وَامْرَأَتَانِ مِمَّن تَرْضَوْنَ مِنَ الشُّهَدَاءِ أَن تَضِلَّ إِحْدَاهُمَا فَتُذَكِّرَ إِحْدَاهُمَا الْأُخْرَىٰ ۚ ...)

> ...and take as witness two witnesses from your men and if there are not two men, then a man and two women –from those whom you approve as witnesses– so that if one of the two defaults, the other will remind her.[52]

There are many issues that can be discussed here.. For example, is it in all circumstances that the testimony of two women is equal to that of one man, or are there some circumstances where a man and woman's testimony is equal? The mentioning of such issues is related to the field of jurisprudence. The questions that must be answered here are:

1. Why is it that primarily a man's testimony is taken and he is called as a witness?

2. If a man is more appropriate and fit to carry the burden of witnessing and fulfilling it, then why is a woman's testimony also accepted and then regarded as half of that of a man?

In answering these questions, it must be said that in terms of testifying and being a witness no right is lost

---

52. Qur'ān, 2:282.

or ignored. It is a necessary condition for the witness to have two characteristics:

1. On the level of bearing the testimony: One must be clever and intelligent, keeping note of all the details with precision.

2. On the level of executing the testimony: One must not be under any emotional influence, and he must say whatever he saw and witnessed and nothing more or less. It is possible that while giving testimony, a witness could fall under his own emotions and neglect someone's rights by giving the testimony in favour of one side, or be poor, or be influenced by other circumstances.

In this regard, Allah (swt) says:

(يَا أَيُّهَا الَّذِينَ آمَنُوا كُونُوا قَوَّامِينَ بِالْقِسْطِ شُهَدَاءَ لِلَّهِ وَلَوْ عَلَىٰ أَنفُسِكُمْ أَوِ الْوَالِدَيْنِ وَالْأَقْرَبِينَ ۚ إِن يَكُنْ غَنِيًّا أَوْ فَقِيرًا فَاللَّهُ أَوْلَىٰ بِهِمَا...)

O you who have faith! Be maintainers of justice and witnesses for the sake of Allah, even if it should be against yourselves or [your] parents and near relatives, and whether it be [someone] rich or poor, for Allah has a greater right over them.[53]

---

53. Qurʾān, 135 :4.

If both genders were compared with respect to having these two features, it will become clear that men are more capable than women. Because men are more competent than women in bearing and carrying out a testimony, the primary person called upon for this responsibility is a man, and the same goes for being a judge and refereeing. Moreover, the presence of men in society is more than that of women.

Answer to the second question: In most circumstances, if a woman's testimony is not considered, many rights will be lost. Normally, someone who has both features is wanted as a witness so that when a dispute occurs, this person can give a testimony. It is apparent that in some circumstances one or two men are not always available. Therefore, it is necessary to accept the testimony of a woman, for whenever a man with those characteristics cannot be found, women can carry the responsibility of testifying. If a woman's testimony is accepted so that her rights are not lost or neglected, then why can't a woman's testimony be equal to that of a man? It can be said that a woman has the adequate capability on the level of 'bearing' the testimony but not on the level of executing it. In conclusion, knowing that it is possible for a woman to forget an event or fall under emotional impacts and personal feelings, precaution commands that another woman accompany the first.

Women's Civil Rights

Question: Why do women have to be given a dowry in marriage? Isn't the giving of dowry like the buying and selling of women and a form of degradation?

Answer: Islam has arranged several economic rights for women, in order to form and maintain a family structure:[54]

1. Nuptial gift (*mahr*) at the time of marriage.

2. The life expenses of a woman are the responsibility of the man.

3. The ability for women to demand wages for breastfeeding, nurturing a child and housekeeping.

---

54. Misbah Yazdi, *Huqūq va Siyāsat dar Qurʾān*, lesson 211.

4. Providing for the expenses of a divorcee in the waiting period of divorce (*iddah*).[55]

Despite the misconceptions of those who oppose dowry, the holy Qur'ān has strictly insisted on this matter. This issue is one of the undisputed rulings in our jurisprudence.

If the amount of dowry is not stipulated and the type of marriage is permanent, an appropriate dowry (*mahr al-mithl*)[56] must be given by the man, and if the marriage is temporary and the amount of dowry is not mentioned, the marriage will be entirely void.[57] In Sunni jurisprudence, setting the amount for dowry and mentioning it in the marriage contract is also obligatory. The bride can grant back the amount to her husband after the marriage is done, or it is also possible for her to give a sum of wealth to her proposed husband before the procession in order for him to use it as the dowry.

The holy Qur'ān says:

(وَآتُوا النِّسَاءَ صَدُقَاتِهِنَّ نِحْلَةً ۚ فَإِن طِبْنَ لَكُمْ عَن

---

55. A period of time during which she is prohibited to remarry.
56. An appropriate dowry is what the general public would allocate as an average amount of dowry, taking into consideration the bride's family status.
57. For more information, refer to practical books of laws (*risālah 'amaliyyah*) of grand Āyatullahs, the section of the laws of marriage, and Qur'ān, 2: 229, 4: 19, 24, 25, 5: 5, 33: 50, 60: 10.

(شَيْءٍ مِّنْهُ نَفْسًا فَكُلُوهُ هَنِيئًا مَّرِيئًا)

Give women their dowries as an obligation; but if they remit anything of it of their own accord, then consume it as [something] lawful and wholesome.[58]

A man who forcefully or by trickery takes back his wife's portion of dowry is something the holy Qurʾān severely condemns:

(وَإِنْ أَرَدتُّمُ اسْتِبْدَالَ زَوْجٍ مَّكَانَ زَوْجٍ وَآتَيْتُمْ إِحْدَاهُنَّ قِنطَارًا فَلَا تَأْخُذُوا مِنْهُ شَيْئًا ۚ أَتَأْخُذُونَهُ بُهْتَانًا وَإِثْمًا مُّبِينًا ۞ وَكَيْفَ تَأْخُذُونَهُ وَقَدْ أَفْضَىٰ بَعْضُكُمْ إِلَىٰ بَعْضٍ وَأَخَذْنَ مِنكُم مِّيثَاقًا غَلِيظًا)

If you desire to take a wife in place of another, and you have given one of them a quintal [of gold], do not take anything away from it. Would you take it by way of calumny and flagrant sin?! How could you take it back when you have known [with copulating] each other, and they have taken from you a solemn covenant?![59][60]

In explaining and justifying this economic right of women, we can say that this financial advantage is

---

58. Qurʾān, 4: 4.
59. Qurʾān, 4: 20-21.
60. It should be mentioned that if divorce was to take place before consummating the marriage (i.e. before sexual intercourse), only half the *mahr* must be given. Refer to the Qurʾān, 2: 237 and practical books of laws.

mainly because they undergo numerous inconveniences and hardships in fulfilling their obligatory and complimentary duties in the family. Secondly, matters such as pregnancy, giving birth, breastfeeding and nurturing children prevent women from engaging in economic activities. Therefore, in order for a woman to receive the rewards of her efforts and for her work not to be without any economic benefits, dowry has been stipulated for her.

The Permissibility of Temporary Marriage and Polygamy

Question: Why does Islam permit temporary marriage and polygamy? Are these laws not discrimination and against women's rights?

Answer:[61] There are two forms of legitimate marriage in Islam:

A. Permanent marriage: A woman and man agree to share their life together as long as they live

---

61. Misbah Yazdi, *Huqūq va Siyāsat dar Qur'ān*, lesson 209.

Women's Civil Rights

B. Temporary marriage fixed to a certain period of time: The benefits of temporary marriage are plenty, some of them being:

1. During the period of menstruation, a woman loses her disposition in being involved in sexual intercourse, while a man continuously possesses this tendency.

2. During the period of pregnancy and throughout most of the time in which a woman is breastfeeding, a woman cannot become pregnant again, whilst a man might want another child. Moreover, to a considerable extent, women during this time do not have sexual interest.

3. There is a possibility that a woman or a man is forced to live in a remote city or another country away from their permanent residence in order to pursue his or her education, business or any other intention. In the meantime, the husband might need a partner.

4. In permanent marriage, a woman's living expenses are covered by the husband, and there is a possibility that a man is not financially able to carry out this responsibility. This problem does not exist in temporary marriage.

5. It is probable that a man's sexual drive cannot be satisfied with a single woman and therefore, temporary

marriage has plenty of benefits. This is especially true when a man or a woman cannot get involved in a permanent marriage or their sexual drive is in a state that needs immediate fulfilment to avoid both physical and mental disorder or any kind of sinning.

6. In certain times, social or individual needs mandate an increase in human reproduction, in which case one man with one woman will not achieve the intended goal.

7. There is a possibility that in some historical phases the quantity of females in society ready for marriage outnumbered that of men. In a situation like this, to prohibit polygamy will result in the spreading of immorality and other social corruptions, and the right of marriage for some women will be neglected. In Islam, no man is obliged to have more than one wife. Practically, since the emergence of Islam up till now, the close to absolute majority of men have practiced and still practice monogamy. But still, objectivity, the realistic way of thinking and the distinctive differences between men and women necessitate a solution for certain circumstances. Thus, it becomes clear that nothing in these laws suggests the idea of gender discrimination or negation of women's rights.

Taking into consideration the aforementioned advantages (except number four), permanent marriage is not limited to being married only once. Rather, it has been permitted for a man –with certain terms and conditions such as observing justness in treatment- to have up to four permanent wives at one time.

It is worth reminding ourselves that we do not claim to know the whole philosophy behind temporary marriage and polygamy (or any other divine laws). There could be tens of other reasons behind this law that we are not aware of.

Conditions for Polygamy in Islam

From an Islamic perspective, a man can marry more than one woman only when he finds himself capable to practice justness between them.

The holy Qur'ān says:

(فَإِنْ خِفْتُمْ أَلَّا تَعْدِلُوا فَوَاحِدَةً....)

But if you fear that you may not treat them fairly, then [marry only] one...[62]

Without doubt, what is meant by fairness in this holy verse is justice on the level of treatment (not to abuse or oppress women in the matters of marital and familial rights), because love and inner feelings cannot be totally controlled. In other words, a man with more than one

---

62. Qur'ān, 3 :4.

wife is obliged to observe justness in the treatment of his wives in things like food, clothing and housing; a man has to provide these equally among them, even if he – based on outer or inner beauty and perfections- prefers one over the other in his heart. Allah does not order man to perform an impossible task and does not request a man to equally love his wives. At the same time, he does not allow a man to unjustly treat the wife he loves less and to neglect and ignore her as if she has no husband.

Verse 129 of Surah al-Nisā' says:

(وَلَــن تَسْــتَطِيعُوا أَن تَعْدِلُــوا بَيْــنَ النِّسَــاءِ وَلَــوْ حَرَصْتُــمْ فَلَا تَمِيلُــوا كُلَّ الْمَيْـلِ فَتَذَرُوهَـا كَالْمُعَلَّقَـةِ)

You will not be able to be fair between wives, even if you are eager to do so. Yet do not away from one altogether, leaving her as if in suspense...[63]

With this, Islam tries to prevent a man's oppression of women. Other jurisprudential points relating to temporary marriage and polygamy can be found in practical books of laws (*risālah ʿamaliyyah*) of Grand Āyatullāhs.

---

63. Qur'ān, 129 :4.

The Permissibility of Divorce

Question: Why does Islam allow divorce and separation? Would it not be better if it was forbidden?

Answer:[64] The holy Qur'ān permits divorce,[65] for example, in verse 130 of Surah al-Nisā', we read:

$$ (وَإِن يَتَفَرَّقَا يُغْنِ اللَّهُ كُلًّا مِّن سَعَتِهِ ۚ وَكَانَ اللَّهُ وَاسِعًا حَكِيمًا) $$

But if they separate, Allah will suffice each of them out of His bounty, and Allah is All-bounteous, All-wise.[66]

There are plenty of precepts and advises in the Qur'ān and Islam to prevent divorce. A part of it relates to the subject of recalcitrant misconduct (*nushuz*) and judging between a man and a woman. But when the conflict between a husband and wife reaches a certain level where neither they nor the two representatives they have selected are able to solve the issue at hand, then the atmosphere of the family becomes a source of misery.

Although Islam dislikes divorce and considers it as the most hated legitimate thing, it does not allow the

---

64. Misbah Yazdi, *Huqūq va Siyāsat dar Qur'ān*, lesson 211.
65. For more on this, refer to Qur'ān, 2: 49, 33: 1,2,6,7 65: 231,232,236,237.
66. Qur'ān, 4:130.

condition where man and woman are forced to waste their life in a family environment and a house that will become the source of enmity and dispute. Therefore, as a final solution, Islam permits divorce.

In the Qur'ān, there are about twenty one verses related to the subject of divorce. These verses carry very unique meanings and are full of lessons. Although they describe legal matters, they are fraught with valuable recommendations and vital moral advice.

Nonetheless, divorce is legitimate in Islam, but it should be prevented as much as possible. When the light of love and understanding in a family is extinguished, the prohibition of divorce will not act as a solution and will not result in anything other than the emergence of immoral and unlawful acts, increase in clashes and other related problems.

Legal and Moral Principles in a Family

Question: According to Islam and the Qur'ān, what are the principles that govern a family? What are the legal and moral foundations of family in the Qur'ān?

Answer:[67] The principles and fundamentals that govern a family according to the Qur'ān are:

1. The principle of providing sexual needs: The main factor that draws men and women close to each other and allows them to form a shared life is the sex drive. A man and woman fulfill each other's sexual needs. This mutual need helps their long-term relationship flourish. Providing this need is the foundation for various family laws.

2. The principle of providing emotional needs: The second factor is the emergence of an emotional relationship between a man and a woman, which brings forth their care for each other as two companions. Allah Almighty has created humankind in a way that when they provide for each other's needs, an emotional relationship will gradually develop between them. This emotional connection plays a vital role in achieving the interests of the entire family. It can be said that the strongest factor of a family's stability and growth is the love each member of the family feels for the others. Therefore, if forming a familial life has any necessity according to the human intellect, the best factor of its strength and continuity is the encouragement of multilateral emotions between each member in the family. However, in the Islamic philosophy of morals,

---

67. Misbah Yazdi, Muhammad Taqi. *Akhlāq dar Qur'ān*, vol. 3 p. 71.

emotion is not the criterion for moral values; rather, it is only one of the motivations for wilful action whose value is measured by the intellect and religion. There are interests and values higher than familial love, such as obedience to Allah and the Prophet and the duty of Jihad that has preference in the circumstance when interests' collide.[68]

Sometimes in family and social life, problems and disagreements occur, and if they are not resolved, they will spoil the once loving and peaceful atmosphere of the family. In order to prevent such problems and solve such disagreements, Islam has given us other principles. No doubt, it is possible that the roots of disagreement in a family could come from difference in opinion, viewpoints, individual interests, or improper treatment.

3. The principle of consultation: The third family principle is consultation. In the above-mentioned disagreement, the best solution is that man and woman share their viewpoint and come to a compromise. It is natural to have diverging ideas, but in most cases, spouses can harmonize each other's ideas through consultation. It is worth mentioning that the wife should be consulted in matters such as how to breastfeed babies, the duration of breastfeeding, where to live, what to eat, what to wear, and so on. But it is better not to consult

---

68. Qurʾān, 9:24.

her in matters that are not connected to familial life. In these matters we must consult people who have more knowledge, so that the matter surmounts to the best possible outcome. Therefore, expressions such as: "Consult them (women) and then oppose them"[69] which have been mentioned in some traditions, does not mean not to consult women at all, but rather to consult them in matters that match their roles as wives and mothers. For instance, decision making in wartime, peace and defence does not match the feminine role, and having women consultants in these subjects is not beneficial. This is because a woman has strong emotions; she cannot withstand the destruction of war and give opinions considering society's interests on a global scale.

4. The principle of the father's supervision: Sometimes, in familial life, some problems and disagreements may occur that cannot be resolved even after consultation. Permanence of such problems could destroy the serenity of the family. Therefore, another solution must be put forward. From a legal point of view, the family, like any other community, needs a guardian. Islam has a tremendous concern for the correct way of founding a family as this will determine the firmness and health of the society. That is why the holy Qur'ān says:

---

69. The Arabic is: شَاوِرُوهُنَّ وَخَالِفُوهُنَّ

(الرِّجَالُ قَوَّامُونَ عَلَى النِّسَاءِ)

Men are in charge (and guards) of women...[70]

In the family, the women and children must accept the management of the man. Morally wives and children must respect the father of the family and consider his management as superior. The solution for many problems in family life depends on putting this principle into action. This principle does not mean the absolute governorship for men in a family, and man should not exploit his right to supervise. Moreover, women shouldn't affray the affectionate environment of the family but rather try to avoid the destruction of the family through mutual respect towards the man of the house.

5. The principle of peace and agreement: Sometimes things get to a point where one of the spouses insists on behaving outside the boundaries of logic, reason and fairness to the extent that he or she only wants to stubbornly force his or her own word. Whether he or she is acting outside of reason , this could naturally endanger the relationship and weaken the family. In such a situation, Islam orders us to try as much as possible not to let the family fall apart; even if one party has to show more tolerance and even to ignore their indisputable rights. Allah Almighty says:

---

70. Qur'ān, 34 :4.

> (وَإِنِ امْرَأَةٌ خَافَتْ مِنْ بَعْلِهَا نُشُوزًا أَوْ إِعْرَاضًا فَلَا جُنَاحَ عَلَيْهِمَا أَن يُصْلِحَا بَيْنَهُمَا صُلْحًا ۚ وَالصُّلْحُ خَيْرٌ)

If a woman feared ill-treatment from her husband, or desertion, it is no sin for them to make terms of peace between themselves. Peace is better...[71]

In disagreements and differences, if there is no forgiveness and tolerance, there will be no peace and tranquillity.

6. The principle of arbitration: Allah Almighty says in the holy Qur'ān that if a couple cannot resolve a family problem through consultation and the danger of disintegration is still present, they should employ people of experience that can be trusted to arbitrate between them so that the problems can be solved. In verse thirty five of Surah al-Nisā', Allah says:

> (وَإِنْ خِفْتُمْ شِقَاقَ بَيْنِهِمَا فَابْعَثُوا حَكَمًا مِّنْ أَهْلِهِ وَحَكَمًا مِّنْ أَهْلِهَا إِن يُرِيدَا إِصْلَاحًا يُوَفِّقِ ٱللَّهُ بَيْنَهُمَا ۗ إِنَّ ٱللَّهَ كَانَ عَلِيمًا خَبِيرًا)

And if you fear breach between them (husband and wife), appoint an arbiter from his folk and an arbiter from her folk. If they desire amendment Allah will

---

71. Qur'ān, 128:4.

make them of one mind. Lo, Allah is all-Knowing All-Aware.[72]

It is also necessary for the husband and wife to accept their decision in order to maintain the family's firmness and to replace disagreement with peace.

The Aims for the Establishment of a Family

Question: What is the reason behind establishing a family and what are the roles of man and woman?

Answer: Marriage and establishing a family have important effects and benefits for both man and woman. These include:[73]

A. The sexual needs of man and woman are fulfilled. As the male and female mature, they develop certain sexual needs that incline them towards each other. In the moral system of Islam, to provide for this sexual need is considered a sacred act. All needs and inclinations in human nature are based on divine wisdom and are there for a particular reason. Islam has emphasized the fact that there are many needs that have to be provided

---

72. Qur'ān, 35:4.
73. Refer to: Misbah Yazdi, *Akhlāq dar Qur'ān*, vol. 3 p. 70, *Falsafeye Huqūq*, p. 219-215, *Huqūq va Siyāsat dar Qur'ān*, lesson 209.

for equally and proportionally in order to achieve a level of perfection for mankind. Therefore, a man has to attain each one of his needs in a way that is neither in conflict with the requirements of others nor disrupting his own progression.

Recognition of this fact requires that sexual maturity comes naturally, in such a way that it doesn't initiate instability or prevent his or her perfection. Therefore, the living environment and human society needs to be kept away from anything that causes premature maturity and factors that lead children and teenagers away from their perfection. After maturity, the way of providing these needs has to be in harmony with the securing of other human needs and not in a way that sexual needs become the sole concern of a person's mind; when sexual needs become the only concern of one's thinking, he becomes a one-dimensional and carnal existent, and the remainder of his needs and perfection will be forgotten. This is a great loss that will cause the plight of mankind.

It is obvious that this cannot be the only reason for establishing a family life, since this need can be provided by means other than establishing a family.

B. Family life creates a mental calmness between spouses. The holy Qur'ān says:

(وَمِنْ آيَاتِهِ أَنْ خَلَقَ لَكُم مِّنْ أَنفُسِكُمْ أَزْوَاجًا

$$\text{لِتَسْكُنُوا إِلَيْهَا وَجَعَلَ بَيْنَكُم مَّوَدَّةً وَرَحْمَةً ۚ إِنَّ فِي ذَٰلِكَ لَآيَاتٍ لِّقَوْمٍ يَتَفَكَّرُونَ}$$

And Amongst His signs is that He created for you mates from yourselves that you might find rest in them, and He ordained between you love and mercy. Lo, herein indeed are signs for folk who reflect.[74]

Man and woman are imperfect without each other and need one another to reach their perfection. This imperfection goes away by establishing a family and thus both sides gain calmness.

C. Family creates love, mercy and mutual feelings between spouses. This stems from a mental and spiritual response that grows when one observes and provides for the needs of their counterpart. This continues as a mutual action and reaction between spouses and creates deeper and more long-lasting feelings between them which results in unity and the strengthening of the family unit . This feeling is also transferred to the children.

In the previous verse, Allah Almighty mentioned one of the human needs that has inherent roots and can only be entirely provided through a familial life. Mankind, especially during the stage of puberty, feels that he needs to love someone and also needs someone to love

---

74. Qur'ān, 21 :30.

him. Therefore, each day he is attracted to someone and when his heart is broken after falling in love, he will seek another. Many youngsters waste the best part of their life in this way and will end up isolating themselves from life and society due to disturbed emotions.

The correct path to fulfill this psychological need and create an emotional relationship is through marriage. In this way, a person knows whom to love and in return he will be loved by his spouse, and they will lead a life filled with joy and intimacy. Furthermore, the deep mental and psychological need is attained within the borders of moral and religious values. These families enjoy tranquillity, intimacy and joy that other families are missing.

In societies that permit free sexual relationships, spouses usually suffer from mental anxiety and do not experience a life of tranquillity. Moreover, in these societies, serious and lasting love generally does not exist in families. Therefore, they will always feel that their need to be loved is not fulfilled.

D. A family provides humanity's need for reproduction and having children. Wanting to have children is an essential need, and in every father and mother there is a paternal and maternal affection. When a child is added to a family, it takes the family into another stage, where new members will form the next generation and the foundation of the future society.

On the other hand, when the members of society expand and familial relationships weaken and the distance among families grow, social values guarantee social solidarity. However, transferring these values and beliefs to future members of society must be carried out by the family institution. The society's future depends on how successful families educate their children. It could threaten the future of a society if the issue of children's education is neglected.

There are two types of tasks that family members can perform in order to achieve these objectives:

a. Tasks that can equally be performed by any member of the family in order to achieve those objectives.

b. Particular tasks that cannot be done by all: These tasks can only be done by certain members of the family. Thus, there is a natural job description that forms. For instance, a task that women can perform in a family environment could never be carried out by men. Women, according to their unique physical and natural structure can get pregnant, breastfeed infants and nurture children. These tasks can not be done by men who are of different physical and mental ability.

Men, according to their physical and mental features, can also perform tasks that women are not able to do. Consequently, the difference of roles played by men and women in achieving family objectives is related to their unique mental and physical features. Generally, we can say that women are stronger in matters of sentiments and feelings and men are stronger in matters of reasoning and expediency. Since the family needs reason, education and nurturing, a job division forms in which men take on family management and its economic needs and women nurture children and the home. Therefore, a precise analysis on family Islamic laws depends on understanding the physical and mental uniqueness of each member of the family and the exceptional roles that each can play.

Family Stability

Question: How does Islam evaluate the role of men and women in a family and what arrangements does it implement to strengthen a family's structure?

Answer:[75] Religion recognises the value of a family as it is the first entity of social life, and it institutes certain laws in order to strengthen this important and significant

---

75. See: *Huqūq va Siyāsat dar Qur'ān*, lesson 209.

social structure. Islam introduces various means in the securing of the foundations of a family, including:

1. The sexual desire must be fulfilled based on the demands of human nature and within the frame of religious laws. However, human instincts cannot show the correct and legitimate way of fulfilling themselves. For instance, hunger only drives a person to eat some food until he is full. But what should this food be? Who is supposed to prepare it? Where should it be provided from? These questions should not be decided by instinct itself. The human intellect and religion manages these things so that the drive is satisfied along with securing the individual and social interests of mankind. The sexual drive can also be satisfied in several ways, but it cannot decide which path to take on its own. In Islam, it is forbidden to satisfy this drive unconditionally; the ways of fulfilling it are restricted. Therefore, Islam's primary step to family maintenance is that the sexual drive be fulfilled with help from the opposite gender; that being said, homosexuality is forbidden. On the other hand, taking advantage of the opposite sex must be limited within the laws of religion. The sexual drive must be provided inside a family environment, and promiscuous and unrestricted sexual relationships are prohibited, whether it be with a prostitute or through 'dating'.[76]

---

76. This has also been used in Qurʾānic terms as 'taking paramours'

2. Islam advises the husband and wife to carry out duties that are suitable to their nature. This matter deeply affects the firmness of familial life. According to the intellect and religion, every duty must be given to those who are able to carry it out best. It is natural that in front of any duty a husband and wife have, there are rights and responsibilities for each of them.

The most important duties that exist in family life are as follows:

a. Pregnancy. This is a duty that is in nature but not religiously set on women's shoulders

b. Breastfeeding. From the aspect that it cannot be done by fathers, it is similar to pregnancy. But from the aspect that women are not obliged to breastfeed infants, it is not similar to pregnancy. It is obvious that the life of infants does not depend on breastfeeding. But all the experts believe that breastfeeding is best for the infant's nutrition, especially from its own mother, except of course in the case that a mother is ill. It is a demand of nature that mothers breastfeed their infants, but God does not obligate mothers to do so; He only morally encourages them[77] and allows them to demand compensation for it.

(اتِّخَاذِ الأَخْدَانِ), which means a friend of the opposite sex (Qurʾān, 25: 4).

77. Qurʾān, 2: 233.

c. Babysitting. Though babysitting is not impossible for men, and in days of illness, death or divorce, they could undertake the responsibility, undoubtedly it is easier for women. Therefore, wisdom demands that this task be done by the mother, and women are also allowed to demand compensation for it.

d. Housekeeping. Although in all societies this task is carried out by women, Islam does not consider this to be an obligatory task for women. If this task is accepted voluntarily or mentioned as a term in the marriage contract, it is better, but otherwise women can demand fees for it.

As acknowledged by all, women are more talented in carrying out the tasks of breastfeeding, babysitting, and housekeeping. Religion also morally wants them to perform these tasks as a preferable and not an obligatory task.

e. On the other hand, husbands have several obligatory and also preferable tasks, the most important of them being to provide for the life expenses of the wife and children. It is obligatory for the husband to pay the wife's expenses for food, clothes, residence and other necessary matters in life, whether she has a child or not. It should be thought that paying the life expenses of an ill, paralysed or unproductive wife is not obligatory for the husband because they do not carry out their tasks of pregnancy, breastfeeding, babysitting or housekeeping. When constituting social laws and assigning the rights and duties of the individuals in society, it is always the general situations that are to be considered, and extraordinary conditions are overlooked.

Just as it is obligatory for the husband to pay the life expenses of a wife, it is also obligatory on him to pay the life expenses of his children.[78]

Because men have this difficult obligatory task, economic activities must be facilitated in favour of the man over the woman.[79] Islam demands the firmness of the family structure and suggests the establishment of a family in which women are requested to breastfeed the infants, do the babysitting and housekeeping, and men are obliged to pay the expenses of the members of the family. Therefore, the religion must do something so that men can successfully carry out their task in providing life expenses and women are not forced to work outside the house. In this way the family structure becomes long-lasting.

---

78. Amongst which is the fee of breastfeeding and babysitting of infants if the mother was to demand it.
79. Even though some women do not have a husband and are forced to seek means of survival and some want to engage in economic activities outside the house and so on, in an ideal Islamic society, men are still responsible for the paying of life expenses and economic needs.

3. Men's share of inheritance is twice that of women's.[80] By placing a bigger share of inheritance, Islam gives men more funds to expand their economic activities. This increases the income for them to support their families.

In Western and present-day societies, they do not compel men to pay the life expenses of the family and under the title of 'women's economic independence,' they want women to have their own economic activities and make their own living. By doing so, they assume they are doing good to women, while this results in unsteadiness and disintegration of the family.

4. The management of the house is the man's duty. Considering that the power of reasoning and management of men is greater than that of women and that they are in charge of the family's expenses, naturally, they are more qualified for this responsibility. Of course, helping, cooperation, consultation and similar features are a necessity in communal life, but the issue at hand is that the final decision that is taken must be by men. The holy Qur'ān mentions these two advantages of men and then entrusted the management of the house to them:

---

80. In some cases, the women's share could be more than or equal to men's share, but these cases are rare.

بَعْضَهُـم عَلــى بَعـضٍ وَبِمــا اَنْفَقُـوا مِــن اَموالِهِــم...)

Men are the managers of women, because of the advantage Allah has granted some of them over others, and by virtue of their spending out of their wealth.[81]

5. Finally, if disagreements and disputes reach a level where hope of recovery perishes, the person who is able to make the decision of the disbandment of the family or divorce is the man. Women can also get the right to decide on divorce through means such as stipulating this term in the marriage contract or by giving back the dowry.

Through these aforementioned guidelines, Islam provides the required conditions for the managing and strengthening of the family unit.

Encouragement and Increase of Marriage

Question: What does the holy Qur'ān say about marriage, women and children? Does poverty prevent marriage? Is being needy a sufficient reason for one not to get married? Is there any obligation people have towards unmarried men and women?

---

81. Qur'ān, 34:4.

Answer:[82] The glorious Qur'ān emphasizes on getting married and establishing a family. One of the characteristics of Allah's elite servants has been explained in verse 74 of Surah al-Furqaan:

$$(وَالَّذِينَ يَقُولُونَ رَبَّنَا هَبْ لَنَا مِنْ أَزْوَاجِنَا وَذُرِّيَّاتِنَا قُرَّةَ أَعْيُنٍ...)$$

And those who say: 'Our Lord! Grant us comfort in our spouses and descendants ...[83]

Based on this verse, one of the features of an excelled and perfect person is to request from Allah Almighty a good wife and children. In other words, the preferable men to Allah are those who, despite their other good features,[84] acknowledge the importance of family matters, wife and children. The Qur'ān further says:

$$(وَأَنْكِحُوا الْأَيَامَىٰ مِنْكُمْ وَالصَّالِحِينَ مِنْ عِبَادِكُمْ وَإِمَائِكُمْ ۚ إِنْ يَكُونُوا فُقَرَاءَ يُغْنِهِمُ اللَّهُ مِنْ فَضْلِهِ ۗ...)$$

Marry off those who are single among you and the pious of your slaves and maidservants. If they are poor, Allah will enrich them out of His grace...[85]

---

82. Misbah Yazdi, *Huqūq va Siyāsat dar Qur'ān*, lesson 210.
83. Qur'ān, 74:25.
84. In the last verses of Surah al-Furqān, some features of 'The servants of the Benevolent' are mentioned.
85. Qur'ān, 32:24.

One of the important points in this holy verse is the use of the verb أَنكِحُوا (marry off those) instead of إِنكِحُوا (marry) which shows that: despite the fact that marriage is a recommended and noble act, He orders us to set spouses between the unmarried women and unmarried men. The expression of أَنكِحُوا is similar to that of أَقِيمُوا (maintain) and وَلَا تَحَاضُّونَ (and you do not urge) or تَوَاصَوْا بِالْحَقِّ وَ تَوَاصَوْا بِالصَّبْرِ (and enjoin one another to [follow] the truth, and enjoin one another to patience), and so on. In all of these verses, the Qurʾān does not say get married! Pray! Help the needy! Speak the truth! Be patient! Instead, it orders us to revive and increase deeds of marriage, daily prayers, righteous acts, acting based on truth and patience, and to remind and encourage one another to observe these behaviours. In other words, every individual has two tasks: first is the task of doing and second is the task of encouraging others to do it. Moreover, it is a necessity for every man and woman to get married, and it is also necessary to think about men and women that are unmarried and to put effort in removing whatever obstacle that might prevent them from getting married. The fact that most individuals in our society do not feel this obligation is because they fail to understand the subtle meaning and intention of the holy Qurʾān.

Everyone has this obligation to the extent of his ability. Of course, this must start within the environment of the house, then in family, relatives, friends, neighbours and then to other members of the society. To emphasize this issue, Allah says that the hardships of a person should not prevent one from getting married. It is not right for men to say: I do not have money now and cannot provide for the expenses of a family. And it is not right for women to say: this man is in financial hardship , and I cannot or will not be a wife to such a man. These kinds of excuses are not acceptable.

Islamic upbringing and education insists on man and woman to trust Allah and seek means of life from legitimate sources so that they can conduct a virtuous and honourable life.

If a person's situation is so dire that not only permanent marriage, but also temporary marriage[86] and even marriage to a maid slave[87] is not possible, one must observe chastity and modesty and wait for an opportunity to get married. In continuance with the verse of marriage (*nikkāḥ*), the holy Qurʾān says:

(وَليَسْتَعْفِفِ الَّذِينَ لا يَجِدونَ نِكَاحًا حَتَّى يُغْنِيهِمُ اللهُ مِن فَضلِهِ...)

---

86. Qurʾān, 24: 4.
87. Qurʾān, 25: 4.

> *Those who cannot afford marriage should be content until Allah enriches them out of His grace...*[88]

Nevertheless, Islam has put a lot of effort so that no man stays without a woman and no woman stays without a man.

Disciplining Women

Question: Why does Islam and the Qurʾān allow a husband to beat his wife? Can this law still be prescribed and practiced in contemporary societies? Is the hitting of women not degrading and against her human dignity?

Answer:[89] Family disagreements and disputes that happen between a husband and wife are amongst the topics that the holy Qurʾān has expressed concern about, and several verses have been mentioned specifically about this issue. Unfortunately, family disputes have been a problem within families since the dawn of Islam, when Muslims were not brought up with a proper Islamic upbringing, up till today. Muslims around the globe are more or less under the influence of material life and Western culture and have forgotten Islamic teachings. This has stripped away the peace and intimate harmony

---

88. Qurʾān, 33 :24.
89. Misbah Yazdi, *Huqūq va Siyāsat dar Qurʾān*, lesson 211.

inside the family. Since the holy Qur'ān acknowledges the importance of strengthening the family foundation, it tries not to let dispute and friction enter this important social institute.

One of the factors that generates disputes in a family is a woman's rebellion (*nushūz*) with respect to providing for her husband's sexual needs. It must be emphasised that one of the most important rights of men in the family is the right of sexual fulfilment from his wife. Therefore, it is obligatory for the wife to consider this specified and established right of her husband and to submit to him. A wife who does not submit has rebelled against a Divine order. This kind of disagreement is not similar to disagreements on taste or likings, rather in situations like this, one partner is willing to act against the law, and that is not something that can be easily overlooked. However, since the holy Qur'ān puts all its effort to diminish disagreements in the family, it does not resort to extremes in this particular matter.

The holy Qur'ān says:

(وَاللَّاتِي تَخَافُونَ نُشُوزَهُنَّ فَعِظُوهُنَّ وَاهْجُرُوهُنَّ فِي الْمَضَاجِعِ وَاضْرِبُوهُنَّ ۖ فَإِنْ أَطَعْنَكُمْ فَلَا تَبْغُوا عَلَيْهِنَّ سَبِيلًا ۗ إِنَّ اللَّهَ كَانَ عَلِيًّا كَبِيرًا)

As for those [wives] from whose rebellion (misconduct) you fear, [first] advise them and [if

> *ineffective] keep away from them in the bed, and [as the last resort] beat them. Then, if they obey you, do not seek any course [of action] against them.*[90]

As you can see, even when the husband isn't given his most fundamental and natural right, he still cannot treat his wife with violence. First, he should advise her with gentle and kind words so that she gives up this erroneous act. When advice is of no use, he should abandon her and make separate beds. If this mental punishment and psychological disciplining does not affect her, the husband has three ways in front of him. He can continue living with his wife without enjoying his primary and natural right, but bearing this kind of deprivation is normally not possible nor desirable. His second option is to divorce his wife, but this will lead to the destruction of the family foundation. The last option the Qur'ān gives so that the family may survive is telling the husband to physically discipline his spouse. Nonetheless, this final way has its own conditions and limits that have been explained in the books of jurisprudence and law, amongst which the body must not suffer a wound, bruise or any sort of discoloration. It must be light and mild. If this could yield a positive result, the husband has no excuse or right to behave peevishly. In reality, the hitting of a wife (with the described features) is prescribed as

---

90. Qur'ān, 34 :4.

the last remedy to avoid the destruction of the family structure.

This holy verse has been one of the greatest subterfuges of the enemies of Islam in order to defame Muslims, lead astray Muslim youth and women and incite hate towards the religion. They have done this through writing, art and scripts for plays and films, aiming to introduce Islam as a religion that encourages men to beat, harm and torture women and to break their hands and legs.

In Iran, during the anti-Islamic Pahlavi regime, many young Muslims lost their religious zeal, due to the destructive propaganda propagated by the embassies of communist states such as the former USSR and China. Consequently, after losing their religious beliefs, they became good prey for Marxism and other materialistic ideologies.

However, we should not overlook the fact that the effect of this propaganda is increased due to our own non-Islamic behaviour. Regrettably, in many Muslim families, men traditionally demand their wives to do certain tasks that religion has never obliged them to undertake. Sometimes they will insult and even hit their wives over such things. If we adhere to religious boundaries, the enemies would not be successful in propagating this sublime and exalted religion as one of injustice.

The Qur'ān suggests the most realistic, reasonable, rewarding and fair solution to prevent disagreement and divorce, so why should this solution not be legal? The same method can be used with respect to disciplining and educating children. Some religious narrations mention that if your child commits an indecent act, first you must guide him through gentle counsel. If spanking is the only way of bringing him back to good, hit him lightly and in a way that does not harm him or cause a wound, cut, or any kind of discoloration of the skin. This is just to remind him that he did a wrong and sinful act which is not to be repeated.

In the subsequent verse, Allah says:

(وَإِنْ خِفْتُم شِقاقَ بَيْنِهِمَا فَابْعَثُوا حَكَمًا مِنْ أَهْلِهِ وَ حَكَمًا مِنْ أَهْلِهَا إِنْ يُرِيدا إِصْلاحًا يُوَفِّقِ اللهُ بَيْنَهُمَا إِنَّ اللهَ كَانَ عَلِيمًا خَبِيراً)

And if you fear a split between the two of them, then appoint an arbiter from his relatives and an arbiter from her relatives. If they desire reconcilement, Allah shall reconcile them. Indeed, Allah is all-knowing, all-aware.[91]

Based on this verse, if the relatives of a family observe that the disagreement between a husband and wife is

---

91. Qur'ān, 35: 4.

increasing in a way that they fear this could lead to enmity and divorce, they are obliged to form a family court; relatives from both sides should appoint a judge so that they can make peace between the husband and wife.

Sometimes the rebellion of a husband could be the factor of dispute in a family. Regarding this the holy Qurʾān says:

(وَإِنِ امْرَأَةٌ خَافَتْ مِنْ بَعْلِهَا نُشُوزًا أَوْ إِعْرَاضًا فَلَا جُنَاحَ عَلَيْهِمَا أَن يُصْلِحَا بَيْنَهُمَا صُلْحًا ۚ وَالصُّلْحُ خَيْرٌ)

> *If a woman fears from her husband misconduct or desertion, there is no sin upon the couple if they reach a reconciliation between themselves; and reconciliation is better.* [92]

The tone of this verse shows that the meaning of 'peace' or reconciliation here is a peace that is achieved by giving up some matrimonial rights by the husband or wife. This means in order to gain her husband's love and closeness and to avoid divorce and separation, it is better to disregard some of her rights.

---

92. Qurʾān, 128: 4.

Miscellaneous Issues

Women's Independence in Faith and Disbelief

Question: Are Men and women independent when it comes to faith and disbelief or are they dependent and followers of one another?

Answer: When looking at the verses of the holy Qur'ān, it can be concluded that the faith and disbelief of a man and woman are not necessarily bound to one another. On the contrary, each one acts according to his or her own freewill, and children are also independent in this matter. It is possible that in a family both the husband and wife could be virtuous or corrupt. It is also possible that each goes in the opposite direction to the other, for example, the wife is pious and the husband is dissolute and vice versa.⁹³ The holy Qur'ān mentions examples for each of these scenarios.

Adam and Eve, Abraham and Sarah, Zachariah and his wife, 'Imrān and his wife (father and mother of Mary), Moses and his wife (the daughter of Shu'ayb), peace be upon them all, are examples of pious couples.⁹⁴

Abū Lahab and his wife are an example of a corrupt couple.⁹⁵

The Pharaoh and his wife are an example of a couple who went in opposite directions; the woman went towards good and the man went towards evil.⁹⁶ Noah, Lot and their wives are the examples in which the men went towards good and the women went towards evil.⁹⁷

Based on the above discussion, we understand that a woman is intellectually and spiritually independent from a man, even if that man is her husband. Women can be like Āsiyah (Pharaoh's wife), who lived in the most corrupt environment, but still maintained her piety and purity. She can also be like the wives of Noah and Lot,

---

93. Misbah Yazdi, *Huqūq va Siyāsat dar Qur'ān*, lesson 207.
94. Qur'ān, 28-23 :28, 73-71 :11, 35,36,40 :3, 36-35 :2.
95. Qur'ān, 5-3 :111.
96. Qur'ān, 11 :66.
97. Qur'ān, 10 :66.

who lived in the holiest of houses and with the holiest of men, but they were drowned in their own sins.

Controlling of Sexual Desire

Question: The sexual drive is one of the natural instincts in human beings. According to Islam, is it free to fulfil this need in any way possible or are there boundaries? What are the boundaries in fulfilling sexual urges?

Answer:[98] One of the human desires is the inclination towards one's partner and the fulfilment of his or her sexual drive. This drive, similar to that of other inner urges, is part of human nature. The very existence of these drives have no positive or negative moral value; what we must do is understand what is the quality, quantity and direction of fulfilling this need. Of course, from a philosophical view, anything that exists (whether it has its own free will or not) is good in itself, but philosophical goodness differs from goodness in morality.

We can understand from the holy Qur'ān that the male and female were created to complete each other. Human nature demands these opposites to be a source

---

98. Misbah Yazdi, *Akhlāq dar Qur'ān*, vol. 2, p. 239.

of tranquillity for each other and to satisfy their drive in a way that will provide reproduction with no harmful effects.

In Islam, the fulfilment of sexual urges has no negative value when three restrictions are observed:

a. Natural limitations. From a Qur'ānic perspective, desire towards persons of the same gender is against human nature and the system of creation. It is considered a form of perversion. Therefore, if someone chooses a way other than the way of nature in fulfilling his or her sexual needs, the fulfillment of sexual needs in this way has a negative value and they have deviated from the straight path

The holy Qur'ān has emphasised on at least three occasions, during the story of the people of Lot who were known to be homosexual, the spitefulness of homosexuality and how this act is perverted from the natural way.

In one of these verses it says:

(وَتَذَرُونَ مَا خَلَقَ لَكُمْ رَبُّكُمْ مِنْ أَزْوَاجِكُمْ بَلْ أَنْتُمْ قَوْمٌ عَادُونَ)

> *...abandoning your wives your Lord has created for you? Rather, you are a transgressing lot.*[99]

The expression 'your Lord has created for you' in the verse refers to a person's spouse. Therefore, a man's desire towards another man and a woman's desire towards another woman are indeed contrary and against divine creation. In verses eighty and eighty one of Surah al-A'rāf, this act has been called an 'abomination' (فَاحِشَة) and 'profligate' (إِسْرَاف).[100]

b. Social restrictions. The source of negative values in the fulfilment of needs and desires is the interference it has with other needs. By analysing and calculating the various needs, the limitations and boundaries of each desire can be understood.

In some cases, through intellect, a person can understand the limitations of each need; but in most cases, because we are not entirely familiar with the interference it has with other needs and the side effects, we cannot precisely determine the limitations. This is when revelation plays its decisive role.

Mankind's social interests demand that his life should be conducted in a family structure and inside marriage. The relationship between a man and woman should be

---

99. Qur'ān, 166 :26.
100. Also refer to: Qur'ān, 55 :27.

under control and within certain criteria. A person's spouse should be a specific person, which will yield many benefits and prevent several considerable losses.

One of the social benefits is that the human race would be guarded through the establishment of families. From this, social and legal issues such as inheritance, covering life expenses, education and other parental responsibilities towards children or responsibilities each of the spouses has towards the other will emerge. These responsibilities should be carefully observed so that the society becomes a positive one and the foundations of human feelings, morality, love, sacrifice and purity take form, while depravation, mental and physical illnesses, the destruction of human feelings and degradation into bestial life will disappear. Divine laws determine the various conditions of legal marriage and its borders; these are mentioned in the jurisprudential practical books of law (*risālah 'amaliyyah*).

Regarding this kind of restriction, the Qurʾān says:

(وَالَّذِينَ هُم لِفُروجِهِم حافِظُونَ ۞ إِلا عَلى اَزواجِهِم أَو ما مَلَكَت أَيمانُهُم فَإِنَّهُم غَيرُ مَلُومِينَ ۞ فَمَنِ ابتَغى وَراءَ ذَلِكَ فَأُولَئِكَ هُمُ العادُونَ)

And those who guard their private parts [modesty]. Except from their spouses or their slave women, for then they are not blameworthy. But whoever seeks [anything] beyond that —it is they who are transgressors.[101]

c. Moral and religious restrictions. Sometimes there are no natural and social limitations. But there are circumstances that become the cause for negative values. Regarding marriage to the opposite gender, there are limitations such as the prohibition of sexual relationships with first degree relatives (*maḥram*) and with respect to seeking sexual pleasure with one's wife when she is in her period of menstruation.

The detailed information on these laws can be found in the practical books of law of our eminent grand scholars (*Marāje'*), where those interested can refer to the extensive explanations and rulings mentioned there.[102]

Morals of Women

Question: There are some recommendations in the holy Qur'ān concerning the morals of women. What is the Qur'ān's most important advice to women?

---

101. Qur'ān, 7-5 :23.
102. Taken from volume two of *Akhlāq dar Qur'ān*, (section on sexual desire in marriage), by Muhammad Taqi Misbah Yazi.

Answer: The holy Qurʾān advises women to observe hijab, as has been suggested in several verses:

In verse 31 of Surah al-Nūr, it says:

(وَقُلْ لِلْمُؤْمِنَاتِ يَغْضُضْنَ مِنْ أَبْصَارِهِنَّ وَيَحْفَظْنَ فُرُوجَهُنَّ وَلَا يُبْدِينَ زِينَتَهُنَّ إِلَّا مَا ظَهَرَ مِنْهَا ۖ وَلْيَضْرِبْنَ بِخُمُرِهِنَّ عَلَىٰ جُيُوبِهِنَّ ۖ وَلَا يُبْدِينَ زِينَتَهُنَّ إِلَّا لِبُعُولَتِهِنَّ أَوْ آبَائِهِنَّ أَوْ آبَاءِ بُعُولَتِهِنَّ أَوْ أَبْنَائِهِنَّ أَوْ أَبْنَاءِ بُعُولَتِهِنَّ أَوْ إِخْوَانِهِنَّ أَوْ بَنِي إِخْوَانِهِنَّ أَوْ بَنِي أَخَوَاتِهِنَّ أَوْ نِسَائِهِنَّ أَوْ مَا مَلَكَتْ أَيْمَانُهُنَّ أَوِ التَّابِعِينَ غَيْرِ أُولِي الْإِرْبَةِ مِنَ الرِّجَالِ أَوِ الطِّفْلِ الَّذِينَ لَمْ يَظْهَرُوا عَلَىٰ عَوْرَاتِ النِّسَاءِ ۖ وَلَا يَضْرِبْنَ بِأَرْجُلِهِنَّ لِيُعْلَمَ مَا يُخْفِينَ مِنْ زِينَتِهِنَّ ۚ وَتُوبُوا إِلَى اللَّهِ جَمِيعًا أَيُّهَ الْمُؤْمِنُونَ لَعَلَّكُمْ تُفْلِحُونَ)

And tell the faithful women to cast down their looks and to guard their private parts, and not to display their charms, except for what is outward, and let them draw their veils over their bosoms, and not display their charms except to their husbands, or their fathers or husband's fathers, or their sons or their husband's sons, or their brothers or their brothers' sons, or their sisters' sons, or their women, or their slave girls, or male dependants lacking [sexual] desire, or children uninitiated to women's parts. And let them not thump their feet to make known their hidden ornaments. Rally to Allah in repentance, O faithful, so that you may be felicitous.[103]

And also in verse 59 of Surah al-Aḥzāb:

(يَا أَيُّهَا النَّبِيُّ قُلْ لِأَزْوَاجِكَ وَبَنَاتِكَ وَنِسَاءِ الْمُؤْمِنِينَ يُدْنِينَ عَلَيْهِنَّ مِنْ جَلَابِيبِهِنَّ ۚ ذَٰلِكَ أَدْنَىٰ أَنْ يُعْرَفْنَ فَلَا يُؤْذَيْنَ ۗ وَكَانَ اللَّهُ غَفُورًا رَحِيمًا)

O Prophet! Tell your wives and your daughters and the women of the faithful to draw their cloaks close round them. That makes it likely for them to be recognised and not be troubled, and Allah is all-forgiving, all-merciful.[104]

The previous verse advises women to observe the Islamic veil (*hijab*). However, Allah also advises men to respect the sanctity of women, especially the wives of the holy Prophet:

(وَإِذَا سَأَلْتُمُوهُنَّ مَتَاعاً فَسْـَٔلُوهُنَّ مِنْ وَرَاءِ حِجَابٍ ذَلِكُم أَطْهَرُ لِقُلُوبِكُم وَ قُلُوبَهَنَّ)

And when you ask anything of [his] womenfolk, ask it from them from behind a curtain. That is more chaste for your hearts and their hearts.[105]

---

103. Qur'ān, 31:24.
104. Qur'ān, 59:33.
105. Qur'ān, 53:33.

The reason for the descent of this verse is related to the wives of the holy Prophet. However, none of the verses are meant only for them. The law of Hijab is universal and for every Muslim woman. Furthermore, the sentence "that is more chaste for your hearts and their hearts" in the previous verse explains the reason for implementing the law, and we can therefore generalise this law to all women. As a result, the holy verse obligates every Muslim man to observe the respect of the covering of every non-mahram woman.

The second advice the holy Qur'ān gives to women is to lessen their mixing with men. Of course, if a woman were to observe the limits of hijab and go to the markets, she cannot be legally persecuted, unless this would lead to corruption or an immoral act. However, a Muslim woman is morally obliged to stay away from non-mahram men and to try to keep her work inside the home environment.

It is possible that special circumstances occur when social and political interests demand women to be present in society. In this condition, women's congregations should be separated from the men's congregations as much as possible. According to the Qur'ān, the mixture of non-mahram women and men –especially when women have adorned themselves- has a negative moral value. The Holy Qur'ān says:

$$(وَقَرْنَ فِي بُيُوتِكُنَّ وَلَا تَبَرَّجْنَ تَبَرُّجَ الْجَاهِلِيَّةِ الْأُولَىٰ...)$$

And stay in your houses and do not display your finery with the display of the former [days of] ignorance.[106]

The third advice of the holy Qur'ān to women is to observe modesty and shyness. Modesty here means one removes him/herself away from any corruption out of fear that they might fall into sin. Therefore, any kind of impudence or weak self should not be confused with shyness.

The holy Qur'ān says, when telling the story of Prophet Shu'ayb's daughters:

$$(فَجَاءَتْهُ إِحْدَاهُمَا تَمْشِي عَلَى اسْتِحْيَاءٍ...)$$

Then one of the two women approached him, walking bashfully.[107]

Through this verse we can understand that shyness has a special moral value for women.

The fourth advice to women is that when they speak with men, they must observe dignity and sedateness,

---

106. Qur'ān, 33 :33.
107. Qur'ān, 25 :28.

and they should not speak in a provocative manner. The holy Qur'ān says:

$$(فَلَا تَخْضَعْنَ بِالْقَوْلِ فَيَطْمَعَ الَّذِي فِي قَلْبِهِ مَرَضٌ وَقُلْنَ قَوْلًا مَعْرُوفًا)$$

...then do not be complacent in your speech, lest he in whose heart is a sickness should aspire, and speak honourable words.[108]

This verse addresses the wives of the Prophetd, however, it is a preferred virtue that any Muslim woman should observe this moral conduct.

Special Rules for the Wives of the Prophet

Question: There are some special laws in the holy Qur'ān regarding the holy Prophet and his wives. What are these laws and what is the philosophy behind them?

Answer:[109] For his unique personality in the realm of creation and according to interests only Allah has knowledge of, the holy Prophet has a series of individual, family and social rights and duties that are only for him.

---

108. Qur'ān, 32:33.
109. Misbah Yazdi, *Huqūq va Siyāsat dar Qur'ān*, lesson 211.

Some have been explained in the Holy Qur'ān, regarding the wives of the holy Prophet , such as:

1.　Any of his wives who commits a hideous act will be given double the punishment.[110]

2.　Any of his wives who obey Allah and the holy Prophet and do a good deed will be given double the reward.[111]

3.　Women can donate themselves as a gift only to the holy Prophet and it is impermissible to do so to anyone else.[112]

4.　No one other than him can have more than four wives at the same time.[113]

5.　What[114] can be concluded from these series of laws is that the holy Prophet has an exquisite place in the eyes of Allah . Based on this exceptionality, he was chosen as a prophet, revelation descended upon his heart and the heavy burden of guiding mankind was placed on his shoulders. What we are certain of is that Allah is wise, all-knowing, and none of His divine acts and

---

110. Qur'ān, 30 :33.
111. Qur'ān, 31 :33.
112. Qur'ān, 50 :33.
113. Qur'ān, 52 :33.
114. There are other specific rights and duties some of which have been mentioned in the Qur'ān, like: 53-50 ,35-28 :33.

rules are without wisdom. But what exactly are these wisdoms, we are not aware and only Allah knows.

Feminism in the Modern World

Question: What are the factors that have led to the increase of movements that defend women in the contemporary world, especially in the West?

Answer:[115] Researchers have presented various factors in this regard. In brief we can say there are three main reasons that have influenced the emergence and escalation of feminist movements:

1. Men's self-indulgence and lust: There is no doubt that in every human society, culture and religious system, women have always more or less been under certain restrictions like hijab. Self-indulgent and lascivious men, under deceiving slogans such as "women's rights" and "women's freedom" tried to 'free' women from these restraints, draw them out of their houses and fulfil their animalistic desires.

2. Economic exploitation of women: Subsequent to the industrialization of western countries, capitalists and

---

115. Misbah Yazdi, *Huqūq va Siyāsat dar Qur'ān*, lesson 206.

employers were after low-cost labourers. Since women had no income, they would naturally accept to work for lower wages than men, and factory owners were ready to exploit this situation. Slogans such as women must be free, they must not be bound inside the four walls of a house, they must have economic independence, they must attend in social areas of work and development, were good subterfuges for factory owners to draw women into the factory environment and economically benefit from them.

3. Use of political votes: In democratic systems that claim their governments are based on people's votes, the power-seeking ambitious opportunists knew that women are more affected by their propaganda. Because politicians needed more votes, they tried to draw women into political and social arenas, and by deceiving and impressing women they sought to reach their throne of power.

Outcomes of Movements Defending Women's Rights

Question: Have the feminist movements in recent times been successful or not? To what extent have the outcomes from these movements benefited women?

Answer:[116] Unfortunately, the results of feminist movements in the last century were negative and brought major losses to women and to mankind. This opinion is accepted by most researchers and thinkers of the West. Below we will mention some of the negative effects of these movements:

a. Women have lost their dignity, have been dragged into vulgarity and become toys of men's lust. This indecency is so immense that instead of men pursuing women and proposing to them (for marriage), it is women that are now chasing men and offering themselves.

b. The availability and unnatural behaviour of women has caused men to lose their attraction towards them. This matter has resulted in men turning to people of the same sex in order to provide their sexual needs. The coldness of men and their impassive feelings also pushed women to seek their sexual needs from those of the same gender. The popularity of homosexuality in western countries stems from this, and in turn, homosexuality causes many mental and physical disorders. In today's world this phenomenon is one of the largest problems that the western civilisations are facing.

---

116. Misbah Yazdi, *Huqūq va Siyāsat dar Qur'ān*, lesson 206.

c. The employment of women outside the house has prevented women from completing their tasks at home, and this has caused problems and disputes in families. Economic independence and having an income has made women more impudent and lessened their fear of separation and divorce. Consequently, the extent of family disputes has broadened. The results of such clashes lead to nothing other than divorce and separation of the husband and wife.

d. One of the outcomes of feminist movements was the prohibition of polygamy. They claimed that having more than one wife is dishonouring the woman's personality and against women's rights; therefore, a man must not be allowed to marry another woman. Another result was the prohibition of temporary marriage that was constituted with similar reasons. The accumulation of several factors such as homosexuality, increase of divorce, prohibition of polygamy and temporary marriage brought nothing other than the escalation of unmarried women and widows. This issue has appeared more disastrous and has become a permanent problem in countries inflicted with civil or major wars .

e. Men who were banned from practicing either polygamy or temporary marriage, when they found themselves unsatisfied with one woman, will not see any solution other than having affairs and unlawful relationships. This increased illegal relationships with girls and unmarried or even married women. Statistical researches by Western scholars speak of this bitter and painful fact.

f. Illegal sexual relationships cause detachments of family ties, deterioration and destruction of a once warm family environment and the emergence of illegitimate and abandoned children.

The mental and social turmoil caused by this so-called freedom of women is not limited to these points. What we mentioned is only a sample of the troubles and calamities that plague Western civilization. Therefore, it is not surprising that increasing activities are carried out by women against this movement of 'women's freedom and rights' in western countries. Today, women in the West are demanding their government to legalize polygamy. They advocate that being drawn to workstations, factories, offices and agencies has nothing to offer them except men who refuse to cover their expenses and requiring them to engage in hard and sometimes humiliating jobs outside the house.

The truth is that even though women's freedom in Western and Westernised societies has resulted in sorrowful, horrible and irrecoverable consequences, it has prepared the return to 'Islam's legal system for women.' The West is now, willingly or unwillingly, attracted to some of the legal laws in this sacred religion. This phenomenon is more obvious in the subject of women's rights; for example, there has been an outstanding attraction towards hijab amongst non-Muslim women in the West in recent years.

With all praise and gratitude to Allah

(the Mighty and Majestic),

May Allah send his peace and blessings

upon Muḥammad and his pure progeny.

www.ingramcontent.com/pod-product-compliance
Lightning Source LLC
Chambersburg PA
CBHW020539080526
44583CB00013B/920